JOSEPH PARKER, LOCAL SARATOGA SPRINGS ARTIST

CHLOE CREEK

PINOT PAIRINGS

Pinot Noir and Complementary Recipes

Northeastern New York

CHLOE CREEK VINEYARDS - KIMBERLEY AND BILL COMISKEY

THIS BOOK IS DEDICATED TO:

THE CHEFS, WINEMAKERS AND SOMMELIERS FEATURED IN THIS BOOK
WHO TRANSFORM FOOD AND WINE INTO TRUE WORKS OF ART

Thank you to these very talented people
for donating their services to create this beautiful cookbook:

EDITOR/WRITER: ANGELA J. CHICHESTER
DESIGNER: LYNDA A. KINNS, KINNS & ASSOCIATES
PHOTOGRAPHER: DOUGLAS LIEBIG

A special thank you to:

STEVE BARNES, RESTAURANT COLUMNIST AND SENIOR WRITER FOR THE *TIMES UNION*

THE CHILDREN AT THE MELODIES CENTER, OUR INSPIRATION

Library of Congress Cataloging-in-Publication Data
COMISKEY, KIMBERLEY & BILL

THE CHLOE CREEK VINEYARDS PINOT PAIRING COOKBOOK
ISBN 979-0-615-533247

Printed in USA
BENCHEMARK PRINTING, INC.

*Chloe Creek Pinot Pairings has made every attempt to transcribe and deliver full- working,
accurate recipes from each participating chef.*

CONTENTS

FOREWORD

By Steve Barnes
Restaurant columnist and senior writer for the Times Union and author of the popular Table Hopping blog

The Capital Region of upstate New York has long lacked a distinctive culinary identity and signature food. Whether comparing against other parts of the country on broad geographic terms or considering the matter on a smaller scale, defining traits don't immediately stand out. Barbecue reigns in a swath from the Carolinas to Memphis, through to St. Louis and down into Texas, each fiercely held regional tradition different along the way. Maine has its lobsters, Chicago its beef, the Southwest its burritos and fajitas. Even within New York state, Buffalo is iconically linked to chicken wings and beef on weck, New York City to pizza and bagels. But in between the Empire State's big cities in the east and west?

When readers of the *Times Union's Table Hopping* blog have chewed on this question, the collective brainpower of thousands of food-savvy reader could come up with no defining tradition and only a couple of possible signature foods: mini hot dogs with mystery meat sauce and the fish fry – that long, skinny piece of fried white fish served on a hot-dog bun, the pointy golden ends of the fish protruding an inch or more beyond the bun on either side. This was an unsatisfying conclusion, not least because, since no one outside the region has ever encountered these foods, much less associated them with the area we call home, they're not much of a calling card.

Over the last 20 years, however, a personality has begun to emerge, one characterized less by a type of cuisine than by an attitude about food and dining. Our better and best regional chefs have widened their influences and in turn broadened our palates. The New American cuisine they create is as apt to include Asian elements as it is Caribbean, Latin or Mediterranean flavors. It's now common for steakhouses to offer sushi-style appetizers, and places with the word "bistro" in their names may not serve steak frites at all, instead focusing on cutting-edge food that uses the techniques of molecular gastronomy and plating as eye-dazzling as abstract art to deliver thrilling, albeit often unexpected, tastes and textures.

This is a national trend, of course, as is the growing awareness of sustainability concerns and the embrace of ingredients that are fresh, seasonal and local. It's this last where each region has the opportunity to most distinguish itself – what our chefs do with what we've got here. Only a self-denying absolutist would eschew lemons or quinoa or, indeed, all seafood just because they can't be sourced from within 100 miles of Albany. But to say, "How can I use other culinary traditions to showcase this August tomato or October apple or March maple syrup?" is to truly think global and eat local. Our chefs are doing that. With our receptivity and encouragement, whether in their restaurants or when we see them at farmers' markets, they'll further define and refine what it means to live and eat in the place we call home.

MELODIES CENTER

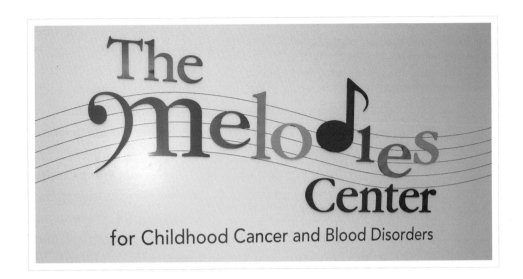

The Melodies Center for Childhood Cancer and Blood Disorders at the Children's Hospital at Albany Medical Center is the region's only pediatric cancer service. Specially trained doctors and nurses see more than 700 patients on a yearly basis at the Center, giving hope and reassurance to children and adolescents with cancer and with a wide variety of blood disorders. The Center employs a strong multi-disciplinary team consisting of four pediatric hematologist/oncologists, a physician's assistant, a nurse practitioner, highly trained nurses, a pediatric social worker, and a child life specialist. In addition, researchers at Albany Med work to treat more children through clinical trials to provide life-saving treatments close to home. With the combination of a dedicated medical and research team and the generous help of supporters, the Melodies Center continues to provide advanced medical care and emotional support to young patients and their families in a nurturing environment. Funds raised support the unique programs and vital services that the Melodies Center offers to children facing the difficult reality of cancer and blood disorders.

INTRODUCTION

"Food without wine is a corpse; wine without food is a ghost; united and well matched they are as body and soul, living partners."
— *Andre Simon, 20th century wine merchant/writer*

The relationship between wine and food can be compared to romantic dance partners – each complementing the other, the performance comforts and the experience satisfies the soul. With that in mind, *Chloe Creek Pinot Pairings* is a collaborative effort between Chloe Creek Vineyards and top chefs from upstate New York's finest restaurants, creating dishes that complement Chloe Creek's award-winning Pinot Noir. I would like to acknowledge these talented chefs from the Adirondacks to the Hudson Valley, who are on the cutting edge of the latest food trends, and kudos to those chefs and restaurants who participate in farm-to-table philosophy and promote the use of sustainable products. Further, I am captivated by the simple sophistication of each creation, which ultimately shines through in a delectable, full-page color photograph. These photographs alone will prompt you to visit these fine chefs in person, who will surely amaze you with their culinary talents.

The concept behind this book – the brainchild of William Comiskey, co-proprietor of Chloe Creek Vineyards – is a glimpse into the world of wine (the nectar of the gods), where Pinots are among the most popular in the world. As foodies and wine enthusiasts, Bill and his wife, Kimberley, are credited with passionately bringing chefs to the table and this cookbook to life. Chloe Creek Pinot Pairings was born of that passion for wine, food and, most importantly, a deep desire to help children.

With the Comiskeys' strong support of Albany Medical Center spanning nearly two decades, it seemed only natural that all profits from the sale of this book be directed to the hospital's Melodies Center for Childhood Cancer and Blood Disorders. Typically a seven-year position, Kim held a seat on the Board of Directors at the Albany Medical Center Foundation for nine years. Today, she continues to participate in numerous special events, which benefit the Melodies Center, including serving as co-chair of the highly successful "Dancing in the Woods" event, where more than $400,000 yearly is raised.

As owner of Kimberley's...A Day Spa, Kim's relationship with those battling cancer began in 1992 when a social worker at Albany Medical Center asked her to visit a young girl who needed a wig. Seeing all those courageous children at the hospital truly affected Kim. She gladly donated her inventory of wigs and accessories to the hospital because it pained her to discover that women and children couldn't afford them, especially since something so simple could make such a difference in their spirit. Beauty may be her business, but Kim's efforts prove that real beauty is more than skin deep.

On behalf of all who worked on this book, we hope you enjoy one of life's simple pleasures: a celebration of good food, good wine and good friends. So impress your friends and family and experience restaurant living by recreating entire restaurant-style entrée dishes in your own kitchen with the help of 50 great chefs. With *Chloe Creek Pinot Pairings*, get inspired and discover your inner chef.

Angela J. Chichester

THE ROOTS OF CHLOE CREEK VINEYARDS

By Bill Comiskey with Angela J. Chichester

"If food is the body of good living, wine is its soul."
— Clifton Fadiman, author and critic

My wife, Kimberley, and I are self-confessed foodies. We even spent a week taking cooking classes at the Culinary Institute of America in Hyde Park, New York. Meanwhile, at home, we enjoy cooking great meals, with an emphasis on a health-conscious diet, and pairing them with interesting wines. Typically our creations use leaner protein sources combined with fresh vegetables, so hearty Cabernets and Zinfandels are not the best pairing wines for this style of cooking. More often than not, I find myself choosing Pinot Noir from our wine cellar due to its versatility. Consequently, we decided that on our next trip to California, we would spend ten days discovering the best Pinot Noirs Sonoma County has to offer and restock our private collection.

Ten days of great Pinots, fine dining and blue sky: It doesn't get much better than that. Kim and I never considered being in the wine business. It was never on my bucket list, and I'm relatively sure it wasn't on Kim's, either. Both of us are quite busy running businesses in the spa industry, but through our travels participating in trade shows all over the country, we have been fortunate to experience some of the finest restaurants and enjoy some of the most spectacular dinners and wine pairings.

Kim and I have traveled to Napa a number of times and really enjoy spending time in the wineries and fine-dining restaurants throughout the area. Napa is known, of course, for its superb Cabernets. Cabernet may be revered as king in the wine world; however, Pinot Noir has been crowned queen, feminine, elegant, complex and very unpredictable.

Speaking of elegant and complex, Kimberley has impeccable taste, so I defer to her on making travel arrangements. She found quaint lodging in the center of Russian River Valley at a place named Hotel Healdsburg, which would provide easy access to the wineries as well as quite a few restaurants within walking distance. So when our plane touched down in sunny California in September of 2008, we had no idea that our real journey was about to begin.

Kim spent a lot of time talking with Tegan Wilson, the concierge at Hotel Healdsburg, who provided great recommendations for dining in the area. The first night in Healdsburg we did not have dinner reservations and landed at Willi's Seafood & Raw Bar, one block north of the hotel.

We were seated early and greeted at the table by Jessica Ross, a very enthusiastic server. Willi's is known for its small plates, and Jessica recommended sharing a number of them. The wine list heavily favored Sonoma-based wines, and our objective was to try as many of them as possible on our trip – although not all in one night. We selected a 2004 John Tyler Pinot Noir to accompany our small-plate feast for this evening. The wine was very good, and I saved the cork to search it out for a tasting at its winery.

The following day Tegan researched the location of the John Tyler Winery, as she had never heard of it. She discovered that the winery was owned by the Bacigalupi family and proudly announced that she had arranged a private tasting at their house on Wednesday at 11:00 a.m. Kim and I looked at each other and thought, really, at their house? How cool is that?

Wednesday was a beautiful, sunny morning – as was every day of our trip. Kim and I left the hotel on our way to find the Bacigalupis' house. Barely a half of a mile from the hotel, we turned onto Westside Road, a rustic, narrow, winding stretch of terrain, which is the most picturesque and breathtaking road in all of Russian River Valley. We found ourselves surrounded by vineyards on either side of us and the landscape dotted with small wineries and farmhouses.

As we arrived at a white farmhouse, we were greeted by a young girl in her early twenties named Katie Bacigalupi. Katie invited us into her family's home and escorted us to the dining room table, where her mother was placing an enticing plate of meats and cheese along with a couple of bottles of their Pinot Noir. While we sat and enjoyed the wine and food, Katie and her mother told stories of her grandparents' venture into the grape-growing business. Katie pulled out an old receipt and told the story of the Chardonnay grapes they grew for Chateau Montalena, used to create the wine that beat the French in the famous tasting of 1976. Sacrebleu!

Following the tasting, Katie gave us a tour to some of their vineyards located on the river side of Westside Road. I don't know if it was the wine talking, but thinking back, somewhere along the way, I must have half-seriously mentioned that some day Kim and I would love to purchase Pinot grapes and make our own wine.

Since we have traveled a number of times to wine country in Northern California, Kim thought it would be fun later that week to try something different and hired a driver to bring us to small boutique wineries off the beaten path. During the course of the day, the driver, who was also the owner of the wine touring company, discussed a small wine project where he produced a couple of barrels of Pinot Noir. During the conversation he mentioned that he did not have any fruit for the current year. It seemed insignificant at the time, but that tidbit of information would prove to come in handy later.

We were home barely a week and just getting back into the swing of things in New York when I received a phone call from California. One of my employees came running into my office saying, "Bill, she's got two tons, she's got two tons. It's Katie Bacigalupi on the phone and she got two tons." I thought, Two tons of what? I must have said it out loud, because the reply was, "Pinot grapes." I think to myself, What the hell I am going to do with two tons of Pinot Noir grapes? Just one ton of grapes produces 60 to 67 cases of wine or about 140 to 150 gallons. Perplexed, I told Katie that I would have to call her back. I immediately called Kim and told her of my conversation with Katie and that she had two tons of Pinot grapes for us if we wanted them. Kim resisted any urge she may have had and said, "I'm not going to tell you what to do." Well, I thought, when life hands you some grapes …

I quickly thought back to that driver of the wine touring company and gave him a call, asking if he was interested in sharing a project with two tons of Pinot. He inspected the fruit at Bacigalupi's vineyards, and he agreed to split it. That initial project was a tremendous learning experience, which ultimately led us to our current winemaker, Dan Fitzgerald. Dan has been instrumental in the progression and success of Chloe Creek Vineyards. Through Dan's mentoring, both Kim and I have learned first-hand the techniques used to craft world-class Pinot Noir. What innocently began as an education in fine wine for our consumption, turned somewhere along the way, into a mission to produce world-class wines of distinction.

WHO'S CHLOE?

Chloe Creek is named for someone very special indeed. Chloe, a gorgeous cocker spaniel, is one of Kim and Bill Comiskey's most prized treasures.

While it is true that Kim and Bill enjoy both food and wine, a few years ago Bill thought it would be a great idea to try his hand at making wine – at home. So he set off to a local homebrew store and purchased a wine-making kit. Bill followed the process step-by-step, proudly crafting 30 bottles of Pinot Noir. After about a year or so, Bill removed a bottle from the wine cellar, opened it, and offered a glass to Kim. "It's really not bad," said Bill. As she looked at the glass of wine, Kim said, "You're not going to make me drink that crap." Feeling hurt and dejected by her response, especially after all of his attention to detail in making this wine, Bill was determined to find a way to get Kim to try the wine.

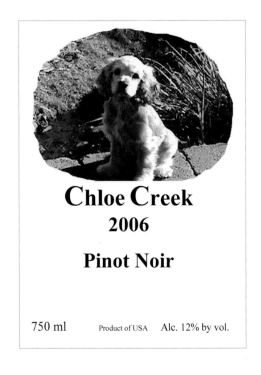

Chloe Creek
2006
Pinot Noir

750 ml   Product of USA   Alc. 12% by vol.

Now Kim happens to be quite particular in the wines that she chooses to drink, and drinking homemade wine was not going to happen on this day. So what to do? In this house, Chloe rates #1, the vacuum #2, and Bill? Well, he rates maybe #3 on that list. Undaunted, Bill was determined to be successful in getting her to try the wine.

One fall day, while in search of an idea for a label, Bill saw Chloe, who was 5 months old at the time, posed on a stone wall in their front yard with a creek in the background. Since a picture says a thousand words, Bill took out his digital camera and captured the moment. He then imported the photo into a laptop computer and – with amateur skill – set about designing a label that he knew Kimberley simply could not resist. He calculatingly applied his label to a bottle of the homemade wine and presented it to Kim for another try. After seeing Chloe on the label, she agreed to try the wine. Although Kim fell in love with the label just like the day she fell in love with Bill, she confesses that, "The wine still tasted like crap." Good thing Bill isn't the vintner (winemaker) for Chloe Creek Vineyards.

Things sure have come a long way. Wine no longer is produced from a kit in this house. Nevertheless, when Bill and Kim began the retail wine business, they needed a name. Bill asked Kim what she thought a good name for the wine might be, and she said, "Chloe Creek, of course." Somehow Bill already knew that. Although Chloe's name still has the place of honor, her photo has given way to a more refined, aesthetically pleasing label.

FROM VINE TO WINE:
FRUITS OF OUR LABOR

Pinot Noir grapes are sensitive to growing and fermenting and vulnerable to disease; therefore, making great Pinot is a delicate and often difficult process. Chloe Creek Vineyards began securing outstanding fruit in 2009 from the Leras Family Vineyards in the Russian River Valley of California. Their vineyard on Woolsey Road has been in the family since 1918. We are also proud to have Dan Fitzgerald on board as our California winemaker. Dan has exceptional talent, as your nose and palate can tell when pouring a glass of our Pinot Noir. With the best fruit and master winemaker secured, Chloe Creek Vineyards is committed to producing wines of distinction.

Chloe Creek Vineyards' Pinot Noir is now available in some of the finest restaurants and wine retailers in California and New York. Visit us at www.chloecreek.com

THE CHLOE CREEK VINEYARDS' TEAM: BILL AND KIM COMISKEY, DAN FITZGERALD AND NICK LERAS

THE WINES OF
CHLOE CREEK VINEYARDS

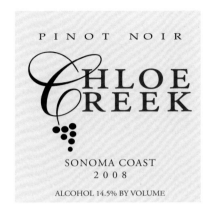

2008 Sonoma Coast

Fresh, alluring notes of plum and raspberry are complemented by a bright acidity making this Pinot delicate and refreshing. Layers of luscious Bing cherry, pomegranate and citrus flavors are accented with sweet oak and earthy tannins, resulting in a delicately balanced complex wine.

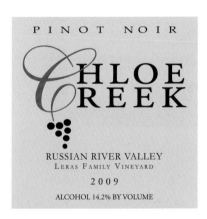

2009 Russian River Valley
– Leras Family Vineyards

Dark fruit, pepper spice and menthol (almost crushed mint) bouquet. Palate has racy, red fruits reminiscent of "Fraises de bois," loamy forest floor flavors, bright acidity and a supple mouth feel that epitomizes classic Pinot Noir. Fresh layers of rich dark fruit and berry flavors are interwoven with sweet oak and earthy tannins, resulting in a delicately balanced complex wine – perfect on its own or with dinner.

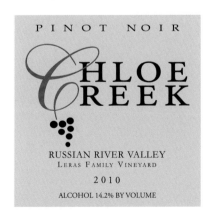

2010 Russian River Valley
– Leras Family Vineyards

Palate shows an intensely flavored core of dark fruit reminiscent of cranberry and black cherries. Bouquet is brambly blackberry and loamy forest strawberries with a little toasty bacon and cedar wood. The high acidity of this cool vintage really pushes the phenolic core of the wine out of that sometime plush, ripe California Pinot style. This lends the wine a refined austerity or elegance seen in only great Pinot years. Because of the concentration of fruit and ample structure, it is being barrel aged for an additional six months. This one's a sleeper that will reward the patient owner that lays it down for a few years. Otherwise, DECANT, says Dan!

IN THE VINEYARD
By Nick Leras with Angela J. Chichester

Pinot Noir is characterized as "the most romantic of wines, with so voluptuous a perfume, so sweet an edge, and so powerful a punch that, like falling in love, they make the blood run hot and the soul wax embarrassingly poetic."
— *Joel Fleischman of Vanity Fair*

Great wine begins in the vineyard. The Russian River Valley is blessed with rich valley soils, moderate winters, abundant sunshine, and evening fog that make our valley the best place to grow grapes and where the finest wines in the world are produced. Fog flows through the channel cut by the Russian River; it's this natural air conditioning that allows our grapes to develop full flavor maturity – while retaining natural acidity – over a growing season 15 to 20% longer than our neighboring areas.

Pinot Noir is the grape considered responsible for producing some of the most respected wines. The name translates from the French words for pine and black, referring to the tightly clustered dark purple pine-cone-shaped bunches of fruit. It is an old-world red wine grape that is considered by experts to be only 1 to 2 generations removed from wild vines. So old, some say the ancient Romans started caring for this vine species around 100 A.D.

Pinot Noir is an early budding vine, known as the heartbreak grape for many reasons, including Botritus, more commonly known as bunchrot. To combat this issue we selectively pull leaves and shoot thin on the "morning" sun side of the vines to get a better air flow and movement. This process of removing branches also prevents hanging grape bunches from touching and is done during the less harsh morning hours.

Since Pinot Noir grapes are very susceptible to spring frosts, which could kill the vine; at the end of February to March, we chop cover crop (grasses, beans and barley which are planted between vine rows) and get our wind machines and sprinklers ready for frost protection. As an additional safeguard, we have sensors located in the fields that will warn us – either manually or by phone – when the temperature drops to 34°, close to the dangerous 32° freezing level.

At Leras Family Vineyards, we're proud to practice sustainable farming by planting cover crops and tilling them back into the soil for organic material and using the cover crops to lessen water runoff and soil erosion.

We pride ourselves in growing the best possible fruit so our wineries can produce the finest wines possible, and we attain this by tending our vineyard vines with all manual, hands-on labor – not machines. Our pruning and shoot positioning, thinning and leaf-pulling and harvesting are all done with human touch and in the coolness of early morning temperatures. It's all about tender loving care for Chloe Creek Vineyards' Pinot Noir grapes.

THE PROCESS OF CRAFTING GREAT PINOT NOIR

By Dan Fitzgerald

"Only when someone has taken the time to truly understand its potential can pinot be coaxed into its fullest expression. And when that happens, its flavors are the most haunting and brilliant and subtle and thrilling and ancient on the planet."
-Miles in Sideways

Winemaking for Chloe Creek Vineyards is more about stewardship than enological manipulation. We source fruit from growers who are committed to producing the highest quality of Pinot Noir with sustainable farming practices. Sustainable stewardship of the vineyards means that the land will be left to the next generation, healthier and more fertile than it was when it was handed down to them. We employ a similar philosophy with winemaking. The grapes are picked early in the morning as soon as there is enough light to pick. This ensures the fruit is cold and fresh when it arrives at the winery just over a mile away.

Every cluster is hand sorted then de-stemmed as gently as possible to avoid crushing the fruit. The grapes are then gently transferred to the fermentation tank by gravity, and 20% of the fruit is added whole cluster on top. The whole-cluster fruit contributes to complexity and structure of the wine. At this point the grapes go through a long cold soak. During this time, enzymes in the grapes begin to slowly break down the skins to extract color and aromatic compounds.

After a six- to seven-day cold soak the fruit is inoculated with a proprietary blend of four different yeast strains. This is done to ensure that the full spectrum of flavors of Pinot Noir is developed. Each yeast strain contributes different flavors and textures, thus creating a wine of depth and complexity. The fermenting grapes are punched down every five hours during the first few days of fermentation, and then less as the extractive alcohol starts to build up. The wine is drained off and the grapes are gently pressed just before they stop fermenting. The new wine is then siphoned out of tank to barrel. This is done before the end of fermentation in order to get a little barrel fermentation. This is especially important with the 30% new French oak that we use, as it helps the components of the new barrels reach a higher level of harmony with the wine.

At this point the young wine is left to go through its secondary fermentation indigenously. This combined with weekly stirring of the barrels imbues the wine with more layers of flavor as well as a rich texture.

The wines are aged for a minimum of nine months in barrel before bottling. The wines are never filtered, never fined and never fiddled with!

A SOMMELIER'S PERSPECTIVE

"Wine makes every meal an occasion, every table more elegant, every day more civilized."
—André Simon, 20th century wine merchant/writer

Traditionally in France for a family that often entertains, a wine cellar of 300 or more bottles of wine was often recommended. By doing so, the house chef aimed to cover all the possible wine paring for the diversified cuisine: fois gras, game, roasts, sauce with pontier, oil or goose fat, cheese – even dessert.

As the host to be ready for all possibilities, within this cellar there would be about 15 different varietals. Today a wine cellar well-stocked with Pinot Noir makes the host job a lot easier, thanks to Pinot's evolution. From its beginning in Burgundy, around 600 B.C., Pinot Noir has had an amazing journey. In the first century, Columella, the renowned Roman agronomist, had already mentioned that there was a varietal in Burgundy with the rounded leaf and small clusters that the locals were swearing by.

It took centuries of vigilance and constant persuasion by local officials to protect Pinot Noir from being pulled out in favor of Gamey (the gamey grape). Pinot Noir has developed new wings and left its nest to conquer new terroirs and seduced millions more palates.

Different winemakers craft Pinot Noir in a range of styles, from light and delicate to fleshy and opulent, adding to the varietal's versatility with food. At Madrona Manor the menu evolves constantly with the seafood; the duck may stay on the menu, but the preparation and accompanying ingredients will change frequently – each ingredient can alter how a wine is received. One Pinot might be spectacular with that one dish, but change an ingredient or sauce, and another Pinot with similar tannin will work better.

The Russian River Valley offers a bountiful array of Pinot Noir for pairing with food. Similarity. Contrast. Complement. When a harmonious paring is found, the whole meal takes on a life of its own.

JOSEPH BAIN, SOMMELIER AT MADRONA MANOR, HEALDSBURG, CA

To decant or not to decant, that is the question.

Wine is a living, breathing entity, constantly evolving, changing and growing. Wine has always been the perfect complement to food.

How do we make the wine more food-friendly, more approachable and more mouth-filling? It happens with the simple art of decanting.

When wine mixes with oxygen, a certain miracle happens. The wine starts to develop and comes to life at an accelerated rate. The subtleties and complexities evolve and improve the flavors often hidden in the wine. For a grape such as Pinot Noir, the flavors of black and red cherry, raspberry and currants explode. The earthiness and woodiness come forth.

By decanting, the grape is allowed to flourish, opening up the scents and flavors, softening the tannins and helping to release the layers of flavors. And how does this affect the food pairing?

Just as it takes time to prepare a great meal by adding the right ingredients and the correct flavors, it takes time for the wine to present all its fine qualities. Decanting Pinot Noir softens its youthful bite, encourages the creation of more complex aromas and heightens the flavors of sweet red berries, plum and tomato. The Pinot Noir wine now elevates the flavor of pork, poultry, fish, ham, lamb, creamy sauces or spicy seasonings that the chef so masterfully creates.

Wine was created to enhance food and food to enhance wine. We can heighten our experience by a simple process – decanting.

STEVEN KAHN, SOMMELIER AT SARATOGA NATIONAL, SARATOGA SPRINGS

Pinot Noir has enjoyed a surge in popularity in recent years, but it has long been a favorite of oenophiles and collectors for centuries. The benchmark model for Pinot Noir comes from the wonderful Domaines of Burgundy. It is here where winemakers show its varied expressions in regional wines, a plethora of premier cru vineyards, and for the lucky few, the wonderful Grand Crus.

After being transported around the world, Pinot Noir has found few homes where it thrives, because many say it is the most difficult varietal to grow well. Northern California and, more specifically, Sonoma are home to arguably the best New World Pinot Noir to be found. The cool and varied micro climates offer similar expressions in terroir as is in Burgundy.

Pinot Noir is often recognized as being one of the greatest varietals to use in pairing with food. The lighter body, soft tannin structure and bright acidity it offers harmonize with the breadth of cuisine that you will find in this book and beyond. The style of wines created at Chloe Creek are in wonderful balance, unencumbered by an abundance of oak, with food-pleasing acidity, bright fruit and a soft tannin structure.

Enjoy the collection of recipes found in this book with any and all of the wonderful Pinot Noirs from Chloe Creek and create your own perfect pairing!

"... Pinot Noir is a minx of a vine. ... an exasperating variety for growers, winemakers and winedrinkers alike. It leads us a terrible dance, tantalizing with an occasional glimpse of the riches in store for those who persevere, yet obstinately refusing to be tamed." - Jancis Robinson

A votre santé,

DOMINICK PURNOMO, SOMMELIER AT YONO'S, ALBANY

THE BEST VESSEL

By Angela J. Chichester

At Chloe Creek Vineyards, we believe that a glass is not just a glass – it is a vessel crafted to deliver Pinot Noir's fullest expression of personality and appreciation of its subtle characteristics. The shape is responsible for the quality and intensity of the bouquet, while the size of a glass affects the quality and intensity of aromas.

Professor Claus J. Riedel was the first designer to recognize that the bouquet, taste, balance and finish of wines are affected by the shape of the glass. His research led him to discover that experienced tasters could be deceived into thinking they had tasted completely different wines just by changing the glass.

While the shape of the glass is important, it is just as significant to serve wine in the

recommended serving quantities at the proper temperature; for red wine, 3 to 5 ounces at 61°. The individual characteristics of red wine require large glasses with a capacity of more than 25 ounces, allowing the taster to, as they say, "nose" through the layers of bouquet. A person's sense of smell is critical, and experienced connoisseurs rely on their sense of smell more than their sense of taste in blind tastings. In fact, approximately 80% of taste relates to smell, which is why food tends to taste bland to a person with a cold.

Riedel, the Austrian wine glass company, maintains that when wine is poured, it starts to evaporate, its aromas quickly filling the glass in layers according to density. The lighter aromas of flower and fruit are first to the rim, while the middle fills with scents of vegetal, earthy and mineral components. Wood and alcohol, the heaviest aromas, concentrate at the bottom of the glass. Swirling a glass of wine opens a greater surface area, increasing the evaporation and intensity of the aromas.

For maximum tasting experience, selecting a glass without a bowl too small or too narrow of a top is important. Riedel pioneered the way in designing varietal-specific stemware, and today the renowned company offers nine glasses perceived to bring out the best in Pinot Noir.

A WINE AND CHEESE PAIRING

By Angela J. Chichester with Sean O'Connor, Owner R & G Cheesemakers

R & G Cheesemakers may be the best kept local secret. Located in the back of a bakery in Harmony House Marketplace in Cohoes, this three-person operation (Sean, Jason Lippman, his former co-worker from Old Chatham Sheepherding Company, and Sean's mother, Lynne Dallas) handcrafts some of the finest and best known cheeses for local restaurants. Foodies lucky enough to stumble upon the products of these artisan cheese makers at local farmers' markets or select retailers understand and reap the rewards of buying local. R & G cheeses have caught the attention of the Culinary Institute of America and the Food Network, not to mention served at the U.S. Tennis Open.

When employing word association, the first word that often comes to mind upon hearing the word "wine" is the word "cheese". With a long history together – some 5000 years – wine and cheese are a classic match. These two have much in common: both are natural products, each created using a standard process but resulting in many variances; and both typically age well, with some actually improving over time.

Are there guidelines for pairing cheese with wine? Typically the rule of thumb would be drinking red wine like Cabernet or Zinfandel with hard, strong cheeses. However, Pinot Noir is a fruitier wine that contains little tannin, so certain cheeses could make this wine taste fuller and even fruitier, especially buttery cheeses. O'Connor believes that cheese should share similar characteristics as the wine, matching tannins to sharpness. His favorites to pair with Pinot Noir: R &G Cheesemakers' Eclipse and their newly created sensation, Truffled Cheese, for its "earthiness."

RECIPES FROM
UPSTATE NEW YORK'S FINEST

By Angela J. Chichester

"Cooking is like love, it should be entered into with abandon or not at all."
—Harriet Van Horne, Vogue 10/1956

Individual philosophies, perceptions and economics have greatly influenced how and where we purchase our foods, from sustainable products to buying organic and local at farmers' markets, to even cultivating our own green thumbs. These changes bring us abundantly closer to the farm and freshness as demonstrated by chefs and local restaurants who now offer seasonal cuisine, tasting menus and wine-tasting events.

Our area is rich with talented chefs, from large cities to hidden little out-of-the-way rural gems. The upstate region, with many New York City-quality restaurants, has fast become a destination for food enthusiasts looking for exceptional, and often sophisticated, cuisine in a quieter setting. Its allure has even tempted innovative downstate chefs to open restaurants here away from the hustle and bustle, cutting out the middle man by going straight to the grower.

As known to many of our featured restaurants and adventurous home cooks alike, our region has its share of ethnic markets and gourmet imports shops, but it is also base of operations for many prominent suppliers of high-quality, specialty and exotic game meats. From Oscar's Adirondack Smoke House in Warrensburg to Adventure in Food Trading in Albany to Fleisher's Grass-Fed and Organic Meats in Kingston, just about anything and everything can be purchased right in our own backyard. Upstate New York is indeed a haven for those who love food.

starters

Pan-Seared Diver Scallops "BLT"
4 SERVINGS

TRIPLE GARLIC AIOLI

½ cup plus 1 teaspoon extra-virgin
  olive oil

2 cloves of garlic, chopped

2 cloves of roasted garlic

1 large egg

1 tablespoon lemon juice

1 tablespoon chopped parsley

½ teaspoon kosher salt

¼ teaspoon fresh ground
  black pepper

SCALLOPS

3 slices thick-cut applewood -
  smoked bacon

12 diver scallops
  (U-10 works best) **

1 tablespoon canola oil

1 cup baby arugula, rinsed and dried

12 to 15 cherry tomatoes, sliced
  ¼-inch-thick

12 cornichons (miniature dill pickles)

12 bamboo picks

½ cup Triple Garlic Aioli
  (recipe above)

Substitution for the Aioli: Add the garlic and lemon juice to ½ cup mayonnaise and blend until smooth.

** "U" refers to under that number of shrimp or scallops per pound; rating of shrimp size and weight in shell – no heads

This dish came about one night as a special at the restaurant. I was thinking about something to do with scallops, as well as a way to put a spin on something classic that everyone knows and loves. The idea began using the scallop as the bread in a BLT sandwich. Over time the dish has evolved somewhat from the first time I ran it as a special, but the spirit is still there.

Preparation of Triple Garlic Aioli

Cut the top off one head of garlic and wrap in heavy duty aluminum foil with 1 teaspoon vegetable or olive oil. Roast in a 350° oven for one hour. Allow to cool in the foil and squeeze the roasted cloves from the garlic head.

Sauté half of the chopped raw garlic with 1 teaspoon olive oil until golden brown. Combine the egg, lemon juice, parsley, salt, pepper and all the garlic in a blender or food processor and blend for 15 seconds or until almost smooth. With the blender running, slowly drizzle in remaining olive oil. Refrigerate up to 10 days in an airtight container.

Preparation of Scallops

Lay the bacon strips flat on a cookie sheet or sheet tray and bake in a preheated 350° oven until crispy, 12 to 15 minutes. Let bacon cool to room temperature on the tray and cut each strip into 4 equal pieces.

Preheat a 10- or 12-inch nonstick sauté pan over high heat for 2 minutes. While the pan is heating, season the scallops on both sides with kosher salt and freshly ground black pepper. Once the pan is hot, add 1 tablespoon canola oil and place the scallops in the pan flat side down (for best results, cook the scallops in two batches). Cook them for 1½ minutes or until golden brown on the first side and then flip the scallops and reduce the heat to medium and continue cooking for an additional 2½ minutes for medium or longer for more doneness. Transfer from the pan and place on a plate covered loosely with aluminum foil.

To Assemble and Plate

Slice the scallops in half widthwise and separate the pieces as if they were two slices of bread.

Place the bacon pieces on the bottom side of the scallop and then a few leaves of the baby arugula followed by the cherry tomato slices.

Top the "sandwich" with the other half of the scallop (seared side up). Place a cornichon on each one of the bamboo picks about three-quarters of the way up, and then spear the scallop as if it were a sandwich.

Take two tablespoons of the triple garlic aioli and make a pile on one side of the plate. Using the back of a spoon, drag the sauce from one side of the plate to the other, applying less pressure as you move across the plate.

Place three of the scallop "sandwiches" on each plate an equal distance apart on the line of sauce and serve.

4 ounces salt pork, small diced

1 large yellow onion, small dice

3 carrots, small dice

3 celery stalks, small dice

6 cloves of garlic, minced

½ teaspoon red pepper flakes

7 Roma tomatoes, diced

1¼ cups lentils

10 cups chicken stock

10 sprigs of fresh thyme

2 sprigs of fresh rosemary

⅔ cup dried ditalini pasta

Parmigiano-Reggiano

Extra-virgin olive oil

Lentil Soup with Ditalini and Parmigiano-Reggiano
4 SERVINGS

Preparation

Heat the oil in a heavy, large pot over medium heat. Brown salt pork in oil. Add the onion, carrots, celery, garlic, and red pepper flake and sauté until vegetables are tender, about 5 to 8 minutes. Add the Roma tomatoes and simmer until the juices evaporate a little and the tomatoes break down, stirring occasionally for 8 minutes. Add the lentils and mix well. Add the chicken stock and stir, adding in the thyme and rosemary sprigs. Bring to a boil over high heat, then simmer covered over low heat until the lentils are almost tender, about 30 minutes.

Stir in the pasta, and simmer until al dente, about 8 minutes. Season the soup with salt, pepper and grated Parmigiano-Reggiano to taste.

To Assemble and Plate

Ladle soup into bowls. Sprinkle with the shaved Parmigiano-Reggiano, drizzle with extra-virgin olive oil and freshly cracked black pepper to serve.

I like to think of the lentil soup as "feel -good food" – definitely my favorite type of food to cook. It is earthy, hearty, and yet not too rich. It warms the belly – perfect for a rainy day.

DRESSING

1 cup extra-virgin olive oil
¼ cup white balsamic vinegar
½ teaspoon Dijon mustard
1 tablespoon raw honey
1 tablespoon fig spread *
Pepper

SALAD

4 ounces organic mixed greens
1 round R & G Cheesemakers' Eclipse
 goat cheese *
Pistachio nuts, shelled and roasted
6 fresh figs
Chives
Fig molasses *

*Available at specialty and
 gourmet food stores

Mixed Greens and Goat Cheese Salad with Fig Vinaigrette
6 SERVINGS

Preparation of Dressing

Blend all dressing ingredients together with an immersion blender or use tabletop blender; add olive oil through cover while running.

Place cleaned salad greens in a large bowl. With a large spoon run vinaigrette around the inside of bowl. Gently toss greens into the center of the bowl. Do not overdress the salad.

To Assemble and Plate

Place serving of mixed greens on a plate. Cut and place a wedge of goat cheese on top of greens. Slice fig ½-inch-thick and stack 2 offset on plate. Scatter roasted pistachio nuts. Drizzle raw honey and finely chopped fresh chives over top of mixed greens. Drizzle plate with fig molasses.

This salad creation is reminiscent of our trips to Sonoma, California with abundant fresh and delicious farm-to-table ingredients.

Roasted Pear with Melted Brie, Spiced Walnuts and Frisée
4 SERVINGS

ROASTED PEARS
2 fresh Bartlett pears
1 sprig thyme
2 teaspoons olive oil
Kosher salt and fresh ground
  black pepper

SPICED WALNUTS
3 ounces walnut pieces
1 teaspoon olive oil
1 teaspoon sugar
Dash ground cayenne pepper
Dash ground allspice

SALAD
1 head frisée lettuce,
  (washed and shaken dry)
1 tablespoon olive oil
1 teaspoon white balsamic vinegar
Salt and pepper
6 ounces Brie cheese

Preparation for the Pears
Wash and peel pears. Remove core and seeds with a melon baler. Cut off the stems and cut the pears lengthwise. Strip the thyme from the stem, and chop the leaves. Coat the halved pears with the olive oil, then sprinkle with fresh thyme, salt and pepper.

Place the pears, flat side down on a baking sheet and roast in a 350°oven until tender, about 20 minutes. Remove from the oven, and cool to room temperature for serving.

Preparation of Spiced Walnuts
In a small mixing bowl, toss the walnut pieces in the olive oil. Add the sugar, ground cayenne and allspice. Toss again until evenly coated. Spread nuts on a baking sheet in a single layer and toast in a 350° oven until the sugar melts and coats the nuts, about 5 to 7 minutes.

Remove from the oven, stir gently with a spatula to free them from sticking to the pan, and cool at room temperature.

To Assemble and Plate
Place the olive oil, white balsamic vinegar, and a pinch of both salt and pepper in a medium sized mixing bowl, then whisk together. Add the frisee, and toss lightly to coat evenly. Keep chilled until ready to serve.

Slice the brie into pieces about ¼-inch-thick, arranging about 1½ ounces of cheese in a single layer near the center of each plate. Melt the cheese under a broiler or in a hot oven, until the cheese just starts to melt and run.

Remove melted brie from the heat, place a pear half on top, sprinkle with spiced walnuts, and garnish with the frisée salad.

The subtle sweetness of the roasted pear, coupled with the earthiness of the melted brie lends itself very well to pairing with Chloe Creek Pinot Noir. The spiced nuts add another dimension of taste and texture.

PASTA

2 ounces dried porcini mushrooms
3 large eggs plus 1 egg for wash
12 ounces all purpose flour
Salt
1 to 2 tablespoons water

DUCK FILLING

10 ounces of shredded duck
1 egg
2 ounces vegetable or duck stock
¼ cup panko bread crumbs

CHERRY-NUTMEG GLAZE

1 shallot, minced
¼ ounce fresh thyme
½ cup Chloe Creek Pinot Noir
3 cups maraschino cherry juice
1 cup corn syrup
1 tablespoon lemon juice
1 tablespoon nutmeg
Salt and pepper

Duck-Filled Porcini Mushroom Ravioli
4 SERVINGS

Preparation for the Pasta

Place the porcini in a small bowl, cover with boiling water and leave for at least 20 minutes until re-constituted.

Drain the soaked porcini, allow mushrooms to cool completely then chop very finely. Place in a mixing bowl together with the eggs and mix together with a fork until well blended.

Combine flour and salt in a medium mixing bowl, making a well in the center. Add the egg mixture to well and mix with a knife until the mixture starts coming together to form a stiff dough, adding a little water if necessary. Knead briefly in the bowl, then turn the dough onto a lightly floured surface and continue to knead for about 4 to 5 minutes until very smooth and elastic. Wrap with plastic wrap and leave to rest for at least 10 to 20 minutes during which time you can make the duck filling.

Preparation of Filling

Cook duck ahead of time by braising at 250°for 3 hours or purchase already cooked. Shred duck and place in a mixing bowl. Add egg, stock and bread crumbs to the shredded duck and mix well; season to taste. Set aside and begin to roll out pasta dough, according to pasta machine directions.

Preparation of Ravioli

Cut desired shape for ravioli, adding about 2 ounces of filling per ravioli. Brush sides of pasta with an egg wash (egg blended with 1 teaspoon water) and place one on top of the other then crimp with a fork till sealed.

Preparation of Cherry-Nutmeg Glaze

Sauté shallot and thyme until caramelized and then deglaze with wine. Reduce wine by half. To the reduced wine, add the cherry juice, lemon juice and corn syrup. Bring to a boil and then reduce heat to a simmer, adding nutmeg. Simmer until it coats the back of a spoon and strain; season to taste with salt and black pepper.

To Assemble and Plate

Boil the ravioli 5 to 8 minutes, strain, toss in 2 to 3 ounces of warm Cherry-Nutmeg Glaze and serve.

The inspiration for the ravioli to pair with Pinot Noir was the earthy flavors of local herbs and vegetables, mixed with the unique duck flavor of local Hudson Valley duck breast. The lacquer of a touch of sweet tart cherry and nutmeg spice glaze sets off the balance and flavor of this dish and most Pinot Noirs.

CANDIED PECANS
1 pound pecans
½ cup maple syrup
½ cup granulated sugar

PUMPKIN BISQUE
1 cup celery, chopped
1 cup carrots, chopped
2 cups onions, chopped
6 pounds of pumpkin puree
1½ cups brown sugar
1½ gallons chicken stock
¼ cup sage
1 cup cream
1 teaspoon cinnamon
1 teaspoon nutmeg
Salt and pepper

SAGE-BROWN BUTTER
1 pound butter
½ cup chopped fresh sage

Pumpkin Bisque with Candied Pecans and Sage-Brown Butter
24 SERVINGS

Preparation of Candied Pecans
Combine all three ingredients in a mixing bowl until pecans are evenly coated. Place on sheet tray and cook for 9 minutes in oven at 350°. Let cool and reserve.

Preparation of Bisque
Sauté celery, carrots, and onions until tender. Add pumpkin, chicken stock, brown sugar, and sage. Bring to a boil and puree using an immersion mixer. Finish the bisque with cream, cinnamon, nutmeg, and salt and pepper to taste.

Preparation of Sage-Brown Butter
Combine ingredients in sauté pan and cook for 15 minutes at medium temperature.

To Assemble and Plate
Bring bisque back to temperature and reduce heat to low until heated through. With ladle, place serving of warm bisque into bowl. Garnish the soup with pecans and drizzle with brown butter.

When the leaves turn colors, the smell of fall just screams pumpkin. Add in local gardens, local maple syrup and the cool weather, and this hearty soup is just the perfect accompaniment.

BRAISED VEAL CHEEKS

4 pounds veal cheeks, trimmed

½ cup all purpose flour

2 tablespoons kosher salt

1 tablespoon ground white pepper

2 tablespoons ground coriander

¼ cup soy or canola oil

¼ cup brown sugar

1 white onion or leek, medium dice

2 ribs celery, medium dice

1 carrot, medium dice

1 bay Leaf

8 sprigs thyme

1 sprig fresh rosemary

3 tablespoons Dijon mustard

1 bottle Chloe Creek Pinot Noir

2 cups red wine vinegar

6 cups veal stock

5 tablespoons ponzu *

PASTA DOUGH

8 eggs plus 1 egg for wash

3 cups flour

White truffle oil *

Truffles always bring out the earthliness of Pinot Noir.

Braised Veal Cheek Ravioli with Asparagus, Truffle Two Ways and Fried Shallots
4 SERVINGS

Preparation of Braised Veal Cheeks

Heat sauté pan over medium heat and slowly add oil.

Combine salt, white pepper, and coriander with the all purpose flour, and then coat the veal cheeks. When oil is hot, gently lay the veal cheeks into the sauté pan, and brown until amber colored. Transfer from pan and set aside.

Return pan to heat and add diced vegetables, cooking until caramelized. Remove from heat and add brown sugar, herbs and mustard to vegetables. Toss vegetables to coat, and then empty pan into a pressure cooker.

Without cleaning pan, return pan to sizzle, carefully add bottle of Pinot Noir to deglaze. Reduce by one-third.

With vegetables in pressure cooker, add the remaining liquids, veal cheeks, deglazed wine (Be sure to scrape pan if anything remains) and stir to incorporate. Seal the lid and set over medium heat for 70 minutes, allowing cooker to simmer and whistle. Cool pressure cooker and let rest while releasing steam. After 20 minutes carefully remove cheeks with slotted spoon and refrigerate. Strain Liquid into sauce pot and simmer on stove top to slowly reduce – do not boil.

Preparation of Pasta Dough

Whisk 6 eggs into a bowl. Separate the remaining 2 eggs, discarding the whites (or save for another use), while adding yolks to bowl and whisk.

Add flour to bowl of electric mixer and attach dough hook, and churn flour on low. Slowly pour eggs into flour, mixing carefully for 3 to 4 minutes. Drizzle in about 1 or 2 splashes truffle oil and increase to medium speed. Empty dough onto cutting board and knead by hand to finish, adding extra flour if necessary. Once dough is firm, wrap in plastic and refrigerate for 1 hour.

Preparation of Ravioli Filling

Add butter to sauté pan on low heat and sweat garlic and shallots. Take off heat when translucent and soft and let cool.

In bowl of electric mixer with a paddle attachment, add chopped herbs to mascarpone cheese, mixing slowly for 2 to 3 minutes. Grate fresh truffle with a microplane into mixture, and then add salt and pepper to taste.

Remove veal cheeks from refrigerator and carefully chop them into small dice. Add to the mascarpone mixture and increase to medium-high speed for 2 minutes.

RAVIOLI FILLING BASE

1 shallot, peeled and finely minced

2 cloves garlic, finely minced

1 tablespoon butter

1 cup mascarpone cheese

1 fresh black truffle *

10 chives

2 fresh mint leaves

Salt and pepper

TRUFFLED ASPARAGUS CREAM

1 tablespoon butter

1 clove garlic

1 shallot, peeled

½ cup white wine

½ cup chicken or vegetable stock

1 cup heavy cream

Fresh black truffle or truffle oil

Kosher salt

White pepper

10 large spears of asparagus

FRIED SHALLOTS

3 whole shallots, peeled

2 cups all purpose flour

Kosher salt

Ground black pepper

Ground coriander

* Available at specialty,
  Asian or gourmet food stores

Preparation of Asparagus Cream Sauce

Wash asparagus spears and chop off the tips; reserve pieces. Cut down the spear ½ inch; reserve with tips. Chop the bottom inch off of the asparagus spear and discard. In medium sauce pot, sweat chopped garlic and shallots with butter. Add salt and pepper. When softened, increase heat of pot and deglaze with white wine and reduce by half. Add chicken stock, cream, and shaved black truffle to pot, and simmer until reduced by half.

Add chopped asparagus spears, (not tips and ½ inch pieces) let simmer for 10 minutes. Add contents of pot to blender and puree until silky smooth. Adjust seasoning with salt.

Preparation of Fried Shallots

Thinly slice shallots into rings or strips and coat evenly in seasoned flour. Shake off excess flour and add to deep fryer, cooking 2 minutes or until golden and crunchy. Transfer shallots onto paper towel and reserve until ready to serve.

Preparation to Make Ravioli

Roll pasta dough through machine until reaching the #1 setting, almost transparent. Brush pasta with egg wash (egg blended with 1 teaspoon water) and scoop out filling into small piles roughly 2 inches apart and down center of pasta sheet.

Roll another sheet of past to #1 setting and carefully set entire sheet on top of filling; starting from one end first and carefully letting pasta fall and roll over filling. Then go to the side you started with and use ring mold to gently press filling into spherical shape, while squeezing out any air. Compact the filling and seal the pasta together, using the egg wash as a glue. Cut desired shape from pasta and set on floured plate or sheet tray. Continue until dough and filling are used.

To Assemble and Plate

Bring pot of salted water to boil. Veal cheek braising sauce should be reducing and warm on stove. Check seasoning. Keep truffled asparagus cream warm and simmering on stove. Check seasoning. Add ravioli to boiling water, along with reserved asparagus tips and pieces, cooking asparagus for 1 minute and remove with slotted spoon. Cook ravioli until al dente. Plate ravioli and drizzle braising liquids over one part of plate; the truffled cream over the next.

Use asparagus tips as a garnish along with fried shallots and shaved fresh truffles.

3 tablespoons olive oil
⅓ cup shallots, minced
12 little neck clams
¼ cup sweet Italian sausage,
  remove casings
¼ cup hot Italian sausage,
  remove casings
3 branches fresh oregano
Salt and pepper
Red pepper flakes
½ cup dry white wine
¼ cup marinara sauce
2 tablespoons unsalted butter

Discard any clams that do not close when alive or do not open when cooked.

Vongole alla Siciliana
(Sautéed Clams and Sausage)
2 SERVINGS

Preparation

In a sauté pan with the oil on medium heat, gently cook the shallots for 3 minutes. Add the clams, sausage, oregano and seasonings to taste. Using a wooden spoon, crush and stir the sausage into small pebbles, while it cooks for five minutes.

Deglaze pan with white wine and cover. When the clams all open, add the marinara and butter. Reduce a little and serve.

Spicy sausage is a wonderful accompaniment for the clams and complements Pinot Noir - not to mention that the recipe pleases her Sicilian boss.

12 ounces block of feta cheese *
   (goat, cow or sheep's milk feta,
   brined or unbrined)
1 fresh honeycomb *
Mesclun mix and herbs or mixed
   baby lettuce, cleaned and dried
Extra-virgin olive oil
Fresh lemon juice

*Available at specialty and
   gourmet food stores

Warm Caramelized Goat Milk Feta with Wedge of Honeycomb and Petite Herb Salad
4 SERVINGS

Preparation
Slice feta into ½-inch-thick pieces about 2-by 3-inches across (3 ounces); may need feta thicker to prevent it from crumbling. Lay the slices in an oven roasting pan and cover with olive oil about halfway up feta slices, and add 6 to 8 sprigs of fresh thyme. Season with sea salt and fresh cracked black pepper and bake uncovered in a 325° oven for 25 to 30 minutes. When done baking, remove pan from oven and leave feta in the oil to cool at room temperature for another half-hour. If preparing feta in advance, remove it from the oil and refrigerate.

Add fresh herbs of your choice to mixed greens (Italian parsley, dill, chervil, chives and basil are a few we use).

To Assemble and Plate
Reheat the baked feta in a 350° oven for a few minutes. Toss the salad in a bowl with fresh lemon juice and extra-virgin olive oil, seasoning with sea salt and fresh black pepper. Place the dressed salad off to one side of the plate, cut a cube of the fresh honeycomb and lay it to one side of the greens; do not cut the honeycomb too far ahead of time because the honey will begin to run from the cells as soon as it is cut. Lay the warmed feta partly on the greens next to the honeycomb. Dress the plate with a little of the seasoned olive oil reserved from baking the feta.

Goat cheese and Pinot always go great together, and this dish – with the herb salad and the other slightly sweet and salty components – just seemed like a natural pairing.

Muhamarra Dip
4 SERVINGS

2 cups roasted peppers,
 rinsed and dry
1 tablespoon paprika
1 teaspoon cayenne
2 pounds walnuts, roasted
1½ cups bread crumbs
1½ cups olive oil
1 tablespoon plus
 1 teaspoon cumin, toasted
1½ cups hot water as needed
4 tablespoons pomegranate
 molasses*
2 tablespoons lemon juice
2 tablespoons salt
(depends upon the sweetness
of the peppers)

*Available at specialty and
 gourmet food stores

Preparation
Roast walnuts in a 350° oven for 7 minutes or until golden brown. Puree the peppers, paprika, cayenne and walnuts. Add the next 5 ingredients. Puree until smooth and add the lemon juice. Salt to taste.

Serve with warm pita triangles and good black olives.

Muhamarra is a Lebanese dip often served in conjunction with hummus, baba ghanoush, olives and stuffed grape leaves for a fine appetizer table. This dip utilizes walnuts, roasted red peppers and a hint of pomegranate molasses, which brings to mind some of the components of Pinot Noir. Serve with warm pita triangles.

Rabbit Rillette with Calamata Olive Tapenade and Wood-Grilled Toast
4 TO 6 SERVINGS

RILLETTE
8 rabbit legs
2 sliced shallots
2 garlic cloves, finely chopped
12 sprigs of fresh thyme
2 sprigs of fresh rosemary
1 bay leaf
3 black peppercorns
2 teaspoons whole coriander
4 cups extra-virgin olive oil
2 teaspoons kosher salt

TAPENADE
½ cup pitted calamata olives, chopped
1 plum tomato, cut in half and
  remove seeds
1 tablespoon olive oil
½ spring of rosemary

WOOD-GRILLED TOAST
1 loaf French baguette or similar
  crusty bread
Olive oil
Salt and pepper

Preparation of Rabbit Rillette
Preheat oven to 300°.

Leaving rabbit legs whole, season with salt and pepper. Add 1 tablespoon of olive oil to a medium-sizes sauté pan on high heat. Sear the legs in the heated pan about 5 minutes. Transfer the legs to a Dutch oven or heavy-bottom casserole pot. To the pot, add the remaining olive oil, shallots, garlic, thyme, bay leaf, black peppercorns, coriander, just 2 sprigs of the rosemary and 1½ teaspoons of kosher salt. Bring to a simmer, uncovered on the stovetop.

Cover the pot with foil and transfer to the oven. Bake for 2 hours or until fork tender. You will know that rabbit is fully cooked when it is easily falling off the bone when prodded with a fork or tongs. Let the rabbit cool in the oil.

When cool, remove the rabbit and separate the meat from bones with your fingers. Be careful of the cartilage as many small bones that are present in the rabbit legs and can easily poke. Two forks can also be used to separate the meat from the bones. The Rabbit Rillette can be eaten immediately or stored. To store, spoon into small jars and cover with remaining oil in the pot. The covered rillette will keep in a refrigerator for approximately 7 to 10 days.

Preparation of Tapenade
Combine calamata olives, ½ sprig of rosemary, one plum tomato and one tablespoon of olive oil in a food processor. Pulse gently. Set aside.

To Assemble and Plate
Toast the bread on a wood-burning grill. If you do not have one, broil in the oven on each side until crispy.

The rillette can be served family-style from a mason jar. For a more beautiful presentation, place small amount of rillette on grilled toast and serve on plate dotted with teaspoonfuls of tapenade.

The Rabbit Rillette is such a country classic. Rabbit farms are abundant in our region - and given their reputation for multiplying, there never seems to be a shortage. We love this preparation, since it stresses the simplicity of living off the landscape. We serve it right out of a mason jar. The olives and the rabbit provide sufficient oils to stand up to a light and lovely Pinot Noir.

BEETS

2 pounds beets

24 ounces kosher salt

8 egg whites

8 ounces R&G Cheesemakers'
  fresh goat cheese*

Good quality balsamic vinegar

HERBES DE PROVENCE

2 tablespoons dried savory

2 tablespoons dried rosemary

2 tablespoons dried thyme

2 tablespoons dried lavender

2 tablespoons dried basil

2 tablespoons dried fennel seed

*Available at specialty and
  gourmet food stores

**Careful beets will dye skin
  and clothing

Herbes de Provence Salt Roasted Beets
4 SERVINGS

Preparation
Preheat oven to 350°.

In a large bowl, combine herbes de Provence, kosher salt, and egg whites until well-mixed. Put a layer of this salt mixture along the bottom of a roasting dish. Place the beets on top of the salt mixture and then completely cover the beets with a smooth layer of the remaining salt mixture.

Place the beets in the oven and bake for 30 to 45 minutes or until the salt crust is well browned. Remove the beets from the oven and allow to rest for 10 minutes or until cool enough to handle. Crack the crust, remove the beets and rub the skin off.

To Assemble and Plate
Dice the beets and toss with crumbled R&G fresh goat cheese. Season beets and cheese with fresh cracked black pepper and sea salt. Drizzle with balsamic vinegar.

Fresh beets are fantastic when roasted. In this cooking method the salt takes on the flavor of classic herbs from the southeast of France. Incorporating the herbs into the salt crust seals in the beets and evenly cooks the beets while enveloping them with the flavor of the herbes de Provence. The earthy beets pair well with the sweetness of fresh goat cheese from R&G Cheesemakers drizzled with tart balsamic vinegar. Beets and fresh goat cheese, a classic match on their own, are heightened even further with a glass of Chloe Creek Pinot Noir.

NAPOLEON

1 eggplant, peeled and sliced into
　twelve ½-inch rounds

12 pancetta slices cut ¼-inch-thick

12 mozzarella slices cut ¼-inch-thick

12 wonton skins

Balsamic vinegar for drizzle

Oil for frying

Salt and pepper

PESTO

2 cloves garlic

1 cup Parmesan

Salt and pepper

4 cups fresh basil

2 cups extra-virgin olive oil

RED PEPPER OIL

2 red peppers

1 cup extra-virgin olive oil

Grilled Eggplant, Fresh Mozzarella and Crispy Pancetta Napoleon with Pesto, Red Pepper Oil and Aged Balsamic

6 SERVINGS

Preparation of Napoleon

Oil and season eggplant rounds and grill 1 to 2 minutes on each side.

Slice pancetta into round slices, and bake on sheet pan until crispy in a 375° oven. Fry 12 of the wonton skins and drain on paper towels.

Stack one slice each of grilled eggplant, baked pancetta and mozzarella on a baking sheet and bake at 375° until melted, about 10 minutes.

Preparation of Pesto (in processor)

Take all pesto ingredients and whirl in processor until paste forms, pouring olive oil through top as machine is running.

Preparation of Red Pepper Oil (in blender)

Blanch and clean 2 red peppers in water for 5 minutes. In blender place pepper and Drizzle in olive oil. Blend well.

To Assemble and Plate

Place one slice each of eggplant, pancetta and mozzarella stacked on one wonton skin. Repeat second layer. Drizzle with pesto, red pepper oil and aged balsamic vinegar.

Pinot with good acidity is a great choice to balance the eggplant and heat from the red pepper oil. This is a dish placed on our opening menu.

BISQUE

1 whole leek, cleaned and diced

1 bulb of celery root, medium diced

1½ pounds cremini mushrooms,
  washed and sliced

1 tablespoon of fresh
  rosemary, minced

2 cups red wine

6 cups of vegetable stock

1 cup of walnuts

8 ounces of butter

Salt

White pepper

White truffle oil to finish *

TOASTED WALNUTS

1 cup of whole walnuts

Olive oil

Maldon sea salt *

*Available at specialty and
  gourmet food stores

Cremini Mushroom Bisque with Toasted Walnuts and White Truffle Oil
6 SERVINGS

Preparation of Bisque

Sweat down leeks and celery root until translucent. Add sliced cremini mushrooms to the leeks and sweat mushrooms until they start to release their natural juices. To the mushroom mixture, add rosemary and red wine, reducing wine by half. Add vegetable stock, walnuts and butter. Simmer until all vegetables are tender.

Pour mixture into blender and combine until completely smooth. Season with salt and pepper. (If soup is too thick, adjust with vegetable stock until desired consistency)

Preparation of Toasted Walnuts
Preheat oven to 350°. Toss walnuts in olive oil and salt. Place on sheet pan and toast until you can smell toasted walnuts, about 12 minutes.

To Assemble and Plate
Ladle a serving of bisque into bowl. Top with a tablespoon of walnuts and drizzle of white truffle oil.

Here we have three different flavor profiles that work well together.

entrees

Pancetta-Wrapped Jumbo Prawn and Pinot Noir Mayonnaise
4 SERVINGS

WRAPPED PRAWN

4 shrimp, butterflied (U-4) **

½ head fennel with fronds

¼ red onion

5 cloves garlic, roasted

2 teaspoon lemon zest

2 teaspoon lemon juice

Pinch of salt and pepper

Pinch fennel pollen (can substitute
   crushed fennel seeds) *

2 teaspoon extra-virgin olive oil

4 slices pancetta

PINOT NOIR MAYONNAISE

1¼ cups Chloe Creek Pinot Noir

¼ cup sugar

Salt

2 egg yolks

1 clove garlic

1 cup olive oil

¼ cup water

*Available at specialty and
   gourmet food stores

** "U" refers to under that number
   of shrimp or scallops per pound;
   rating of shrimp size and weight in
   shell – no heads

Preparation of the Shrimp

Peel and devein shrimp. Butterfly each and season with salt and pepper. As thinly as possible, shave ½ head of fennel bulb, keeping some of the green tops (These are called fennel fronds and resemble fresh dill). Try using a mandoline on fennel.

Place shaved fennel and red onion into a mixing bowl and add 5 roasted garlic cloves. To make your own roasted garlic, roast a whole head of garlic drizzled with 1 tablespoon of oil and wrap in foil and bake in oven, or slowly cook in oil in a sauté pan until soft and semi-golden brown.

Microplane 2 teaspoons of lemon zest and then squeeze 2 teaspoons of lemon juice into the fennel mixture. Add salt and pepper, pinch of fennel pollen and extra-virgin olive oil to the same mixture. Crush together all ingredients with your hands to try to extract all flavors. Fill the center of the shrimp with the "slaw" type mixture and close.

Meanwhile, lay out pancetta slices. Wrap around shrimp as tightly as possible to ensure that when it cooks, the pancetta shrinks around the shrimp. Sear in a hot pan, flip over and finish in a 350° oven. Bake until golden brown.

Preparation of Pinot Noir Mayonnaise

Reduce Pinot Noir in saucepan with sugar; carefully reduce until almost syrup-like but not too far. Let this cool at room temperature.

In blender or food processor add egg yolks, Pinot Noir reduction, garlic, salt, pepper and water. Turn on blender and start drizzling in oil slowly to start emulsifying and thickening.

To Assemble and Plate

Take a spoonful of mayonnaise and place on plate. With the back of spoon, drag just a bit. Put rested shrimp on top of mayonnaise and garnish with fronds.

My inspiration for this dish comes from my early twenties, when I started to take cooking seriously. We had a dish on the menu that revolved around red wine mayonnaise, prawns, and brown butter. I still remember how much I enjoyed how the mayonnaise complemented the shrimp, so I thought I would re-invent it in a new way with pancetta, shaved fennel, and lemon. Good stuff.

MUSHROOM DEMI-GLAZE
1 pound dried porcini mushrooms
1 bunch fresh asparagus,
  roughly chopped
10 cloves garlic, peeled
2½ gallons of water

GEORGE HARRISON
1 pound assorted mushrooms
½ cup Marsala wine
½ cup Mushroom Demi-Glaze
  (recipe above) or store-bought
  mushroom gravy
1 pound of mushroom ravioli
  or pasta

BRUSCHETTA
2 slices thick-cut Italian bread
2 plum tomatoes, diced
6 leaves fresh basil, chopped
3 cloves garlic, chopped
4 ounces shredded
  mozzarella cheese
Extra virgin-olive oil

George Harrison
(Fresh Assorted Sautéed Mushrooms in a Marsala Wine-Porcini Mushroom Demi-Glaze Sauce over Wild Mushroom Ravioli)
4 SERVINGS

Preparation of Demi-Glaze
Combine all ingredients for demi-glaze in a large pot and bring to a boil. Turn heat down and simmer for 2½ to 3 hours. Strain liquid into another pot and return to stove. Bring strained liquid to a boil and reduce heat and simmer until liquid is reduced by half or is the consistency of gravy. Recipe yields 3 quarts of demi-glaze. Freeze for other sauces.

Preparation of Mushroom-Wine Sauce
While slicing the mushrooms, bring a pot of water to a boil for the raviolis or pasta.

In sauce pan, add sliced mushrooms, Marsala wine and demi-glaze or mushroom gravy. Sauté on medium-high heat until mushrooms are tender.

To Assemble and Plate
Top bread with a drizzle of extra-virgin olive oil, diced tomatoes, garlic and shredded mozzarella. Bake bread in a 375° oven until cheese is melted. Remove from oven and top with the fresh chopped basil.

Cook the ravioli or pasta according to directions, drain and top with mushroom-wine sauce. Serve immediately with bruschetta and a glass of wine.

The pairing of mushrooms and Pinot Noir is a perfect fit. Mushrooms reveal terroir (a wine growing environment, covering soil, site and local climate) just as Pinot Noir shows terroir, a match made in heaven. With the combined taste of garlic, tomatoes, cheese and fresh basil from the bruschetta, the flavors of Pinot Noir jump out of the glass. This is an easy and delightful pairing combination – full of flavor and nuance.

STUFFING

12 slices of prosciutto, julienned

1 yellow onion, finely diced

3 stalks of celery, finely diced

8 black mission figs, cut
  into quarters

4 sprigs fresh rosemary,
  finely chopped

¼ cup of Port

10 cloves of garlic, minced

One loaf of Italian bread,
  pulled into bite sized pieces

Chicken stock

Extra-virgin olive oil

Salt and pepper

2 Cornish game hens

ROASTED CIPOLLINI ONIONS

20 cipollini onions, skin on

Extra-virgin olive oil

Salt and pepper

Sugar

FIGS

8 black mission figs

Extra-virgin olive oil

Salt and pepper

CREAMED SPINACH

2 bags baby spinach, cleaned

2 cups heavy cream

Parmigiano-Reggiano rind

Nutmeg

Salt and pepper

The stuffed Cornish game hen has that perfect sweet-salty flavor combination that I often strive for. Figs are one of my very favorite ingredients to work with because of their versatility. I feel this recipe showcases the fig – so subtle and yet so complex.

Cornish Game Hens with Fresh Fig and Prosciutto Stuffing, Creamed Spinach, Roasted Cipollini Onions and Grilled Figs
2 SERVINGS

Preparation of the Stuffing

Put a small amount of extra-virgin olive oil and prosciutto into a sauté pan. Cook until crispy. Remove the prosciutto from the pan and set aside.

Add a small amount of olive oil to the pan, adding onions and celery and cooking until vegetables are translucent. Add the cut figs, rosemary and Port wine to the vegetables. Cook until figs begin to soften but do not lose their shape. Add two to three heaping spoonfuls of minced garlic to the mixture. Return the cooked prosciutto to the pan. Taste and adjust seasoning appropriately with salt and freshly cracked black pepper.

Place the pulled pieces of Italian bread in a large bowl and pour the vegetable-fig mixture over the top. Stir to combine with a wooden spoon. Add ¼ cup of warm chicken stock, and then 2 tablespoons of extra-virgin olive oil. Continue adding stock, a ¼ cup at a time until the stuffing reaches desired wetness.

Thoroughly rinse game hens with cold water on the outside, as well as inside the cavity. Pat dry and place on a sheet tray propped up on a roasting rack. Drizzle the hens with extra-virgin olive oil and season generously with salt, fresh cracked pepper and finely chopped thyme. Stuff the cavity with fig-procuitto stuffing until it is slightly overflowing.

Hens should take approximately one hour to cook, breast side up in a 375° oven. Hens are done if juices run clear when thigh pricked with toothpick.

Preparation of Roasted Cipollini Onions

On a sheet tray, drizzle onions with olive oil, salt, pepper and a little sugar. Roast until soft in a 375° oven. When soft, pop them out of the skins.

Preparation of Figs

Cut figs in half, drizzle with olive oil, salt and pepper and grill over flame until grill marks appear on flat side.

Preparation for Creamed Spinach

Steam spinach for 2 minutes or until wilted. Shock in an ice bath. Remove spinach from ice bath and squeeze out excess water. Very finely chop the spinach. In a sauce pan over medium to medium low heat, warm and reduce heavy cream with Parmesan rind. Remove from heat when heavy cream is thick enough to coat the back of a spoon. Remove rind and season spinach with salt, pepper and ground nutmeg. In a sauté pan, warm chopped spinach with heavy cream mixture until it reaches desired creaminess.

To Assemble and Plate

On a serving plate, place one cooked, stuffed game hen on a bed of spinach. Place a serving of onions and grilled figs alongside.

4 pounds fresh rabbit, cut
  into 10 pieces
1 cup white vinegar
1 cup extra-virgin olive oil
3 large Spanish onions, chopped
10 cloves garlic, chopped
3 tablespoons tomato paste
2 cups Chloe Creek Pinot Noir
2 tablespoons red wine vinegar
3 bay leaves
1 tablespoon fresh rosemary
1 tablespoon fresh sage
1 tablespoon cumin
1 cinnamon stick
5 cups water
3 pounds small white onions, peeled

Lago Stefatho (Rabbit Stew)
8 SERVINGS

Preparation

In a large stock pot over medium heat, boil rabbit and white vinegar for 10 minutes, then drain and rinse rabbit under cold running water.

In a stock pot over low heat, sauté chopped onion and garlic with extra-virgin olive oil until soft. Add rabbit, and continue to sauté for 10 minutes, then add all remaining ingredients - except the small white onions, and continue cooking for 20 to 30 minutes. Add the small white onions and continue to cook an additional 30 minutes.

Stew can be made in advance and kept refrigerated in a covered container until ready to serve. Reheat on the range top over low heat.

To Assemble and Plate

Serve rabbit stew with white or brown rice or Pilaf.

Lean, healthy rabbit is not well-suited for roasting or grilling; but rather stewing with wine, chicken stock, and vegetables, which brings out its natural flavors, and mellows its gaminess.

Chloe Creek Pinot Noir's earthiness, combined with its vibrant berry qualities, is the perfect paring – both for cooking and drinking.

Saba Marinated Quail with Butternut Squash Gratin
8 SERVINGS

MARINADE

24 hours in advance

2 shallots, diced

2 tablespoons thyme, chopped

2 tablespoons sage, chopped

2 tablespoons parsley, chopped

6 ounces extra-virgin olive oil

Salt and pepper

3 ounces saba or balsamic *

16 quails (2 quails per serving)
  The quails come sleeved - just clip
  the wing tips and season with salt
  and pepper

SQUASH GRATIN

2 ounces pancetta, diced

1 leek, diced

1 cup of heavy cream

1 large butternut squash, diced
 (6 cups)

2 tablespoon fresh sage, chiffonade

¾ cup grated Parmesan

1 cup bread crumbs

Salt and pepper

*Available at specialty, Asian and
  gourmet food stores

Preparation of Gratin
In sauté pan on medium heat, render pancetta until golden brown. Discard excess fat; then add leeks and sweat until translucent but not brown. Add heavy cream and bring to simmer.

In mixing bowl, add squash, cream mixture, cheese, sage, salt and pepper. Mix together thoroughly and put in earthen pan. Sprinkle breadcrumbs over top and bake in a 375° oven for 30 to 45 minutes until top browns and squash is tender.

Preparation of Quail
Grill quail until golden brown, plump and tender, approximately 5 minutes (Be careful not to overcook).

To Assemble and Plate
For each serving, place 2 quails decoratively over warm gratin and finish with a drizzle of saba. Add some steamed greens for additional color.

The delicate flavors of quail complemented by a slightly acidic nature of the saba provide a perfect background for the complexity and low level of tannins in Pinot Noir.

PASTA

4 cups flour

3 whole eggs

1 yolk

1 tablespoon extra-virgin olive oil

Salt and pepper

BOAR RAGU

5 pounds boar shoulder
  (boned, rolled and tied)

2 medium onions, diced small

1 large carrot, diced small

3 celery ribs, diced small

8 ounces tomato paste

½ bottle Chloe Creek Pinot Noir

2 quarts veal stock

Sachet of thyme, peppercorns,
  bay leaves, parsley stems and
  garlic wrapped in cheesecloth

Butter

Salt and pepper

Cinghale all Papparadelle (Wild Boar Ragu)
10 TO 12 SERVINGS

Preparation of Pasta

Place flour on clean, smooth surface, forming into a well. With a fork, mix eggs, oil, salt and pepper and yolk; pour into center of flour well. Slowly mix flour into egg mixture, pulling small amounts from the sides of the well as you mix. When flour is fully incorporated, form into a ball and knead 10 minutes until the dough feels firm and bounces back when poked lightly. Cover loosely with plastic wrap and let rest 30 minutes at room temperature or 1 to 2 hours in refrigerator. Roll dough to 1/16-inch thickness and cut into sheets. Cut sheets into 1½- to 2-inch ribbons. Toss with flour and set aside.

Preparation of Ragu

Preheat oven to 300°.

Generously season boar shoulder on all sides with salt and pepper. In skillet with oil, brown boar for 8 to 10 minutes on each side. Remove from pot. Sweat chopped mirepoix (onion, celery and carrot) in remaining fat until fragrant and soft. Season and add tomato paste with mirepoix , cooking about 10 to 15 minutes, taking care not to burn. Deglaze pan with Pinot Noir. Bring to a boil and then simmer 5 minutes to reduce slightly. Add stock, bring to a boil. Season lightly.

Add boar and sachet, cover and place in oven 2 to 2½ hours until meat falls apart. Cool. Shred boar meat. Strain solids out of stock, skim all fat. Reduce liquid by one-half, add boar meat, and adjust seasonings. Mount with butter.

To Assemble and Plate

In a pot of boiling, salted water, cook pasta for 3 to 5 minutes or until tender. Strain pasta and toss with ragu. Season with grated Parmigiano-Reggiano.

Plate tossed pasta and ragu. Garnish finished dish with chopped fresh parsley and more Parmigiano-Reggiano.

The weight and body of Pinot Noir tend to be light and thin in the mouth, balancing this lighter juiciness with the minimal juiciness of leaner meats such as wild game meats and in particular wild boar. In addition, the subtle tannins in pinot noir allow for more subtlety to show through in the boar. Further, the inherent gaminess of a well balanced Pinot Noir complements the earthy flavors of the boar, thyme and bay leaves in the recipe. In a final note, what better pairing for any wine than a dish cooked with that wine!

Filet Mignon "Cheese Steak" Wellington
4 SERVINGS

WELLINGTON
Four 8-ounce filet mignon steaks
1 sheet puff pastry
4 slices sharp cheddar cheese
Salt and pepper

SWEET PEPPER COMPOTE
1 yellow onion
3 red bell peppers
2 cloves garlic, chopped
1 tablespoon smoked paprika
¼ cup extra-virgin olive oil
8 button mushrooms

Preparation of Pastry
Preheat oven to 400°.

Cut out four, 4-inch circles. Place on cookie sheet and bake in 400° oven for 12 minutes, or until pastry has risen and is golden brown.

Preparation of Compote
Slice onion thinly. Halve peppers, scrape out seeds and slice thinly. Heat extra-virgin olive oil in sauce pan over medium heat. Add onions, sweating until translucent, about 8 minutes. Add garlic, peppers, and smoked paprika. Cover and cook on low heat for 30 minutes, stirring occasionally.

Preparation of Steak
Heat a sauté pan until very hot. Sprinkle steaks liberally with salt and pepper. Add steaks to pan and let sear on one side for 4 minutes, then flip steak and put in a 400° oven 6 minutes for medium rare. Meanwhile slice mushrooms. Take steaks out of oven, and put on plate to rest. Add mushrooms to same pan, cooking for 5 minutes. Take the mushrooms and add to pepper mixture. Season mixture with salt and pepper.

To Assemble and Plate
Top each steak with pepper-mushroom mixture and one slice of cheese, return to oven just to melt cheese. Slice each pastry, horizontally in half; place steak on bottom half, cover with top half and place on serving plate.

Chloe Creek's Pinot Noir is a perfect complement to filet mignon done in this manner. Roasted beef, earthy mushrooms, sweet bell peppers and smoked paprika, along with cheddar cheese makes a great foil to show off this well-rounded Pinot Noir.

Faraona con Pinot e Ciliege
(Guinea Hen Porchetta-Style, Filled with Cherries and Pinot Noir for Roasting)
4 SERVINGS

Note: De-bone bird for porchetta-style

One 3-pound guinea hen
1 cup Chloe Creek Pinot Noir
Soy oil

STOCK
Make day ahead
Reserved bones
1 onion, peeled and halved
2 carrots, peeled
4 ribs of celery, halved widthwise
2 bay leaves

WINE REDUCTION
1 bottle Chloe Creek Pinot Noir
1 shallot
⅔ cup dried cherries
2 ounces butter

SEASONING MIX
1 sprig of rosemary
5 leaves of sage
1 sprig of thyme
10 fennel seeds
⅔ teaspoon salt
½ clove of garlic

FOR STUFFING BIRD
⅓ cup dried cherries
1 handful fresh cherries, pitted
6 ounces beef tenderloin
10 slices of cured lard
Salt and pepper

The hen is provided by Wannabea Rabbitry and our dear friend Bruce Marchegian. The lard is a house product and it is from a locally eased "mule foot" hog of Ariel's Farm in Wilton-Gansevoort area. The filet is Australian grass fed.

Preparation of Guinea Hen
Cut the back bone off the bird and reserve. Proceed to debone the hen entirely and preserve all the bones to roast for the stock.

Preparation of Stock
Roast the bones in a 350° oven for 15 to 20 minutes until deep golden brown.

Prepare the onion, carrots and celery. Fill a stock pot with water. Add all the bones and vegetables and bay leaves. Let boil and reduce for 3 hours. (This part should be made a day ahead).

Preparation of Wine Reduction
In a sauce pan, pour 1 bottle of Pinot Noir, add the ⅔ cup of the dried cherries and the shallot. Let reduce to one-third, approx 1 hour. When done blend with immersion blender. Strain the hen stock then add the wine reduction to the stock, reducing further to one-third of the volume. Set aside to cool.

To Stuff the Bird
Lay the bird vestige on the cutting board skin down, seasoning lightly with salt and pepper.

Harvest all the leaves from the rosemary, thyme and blend in a food processor along with sage, the fennel seeds and ⅔ teaspoon of salt. Finally add the garlic to create seasoning mix. Lay 6 slices of lard on the bird then cut the beef tenderloin into strips and do the same. Use the seasoning mix, sprinkle and distribute evenly on the meat.

Rehydrate the remaining ⅓ cup cherries with warm water, clean then lay a line of cherries down the center of the bird. Pit some fresh cherries and do the same.

Roll the bird starting from the top to form the typical porchetta shape. Using butcher twine, tie bird in the roast fashion. Remaining lard lies on top of the finished product.

Prepare the nonstick roasting pan or skillet. Pour just few drops of soy oil on the bottom of the pan, lay the porchetta in the pan and place in a 350° oven. After 10 minutes, pour a glass of Pinot Noir in the pan, carefully close the door and let roast for 10 additional minutes.

Flip the bird to color evenly, letting hen roast until done. Flip one more time. Internal temperature can be checked; it has to reach 165° (170°will not be a problem).

To Assemble and Plate
Finish the wine reduction in sauce pan with 2 ounces of butter, reducing until bubbly. Let the porchetta rest and then slice. Use the glaze to color the serving plate and then lay the hen slices on top for presentation.

DUCK CONFIT

24 hours ahead

4 whole duck legs
  (with thighs, skin intact)
8 cloves garlic, peeled
1 shallot, peeled and sliced
6 sprigs fresh thyme
3 sprigs fresh rosemary
2 teaspoons coarse ground
  black pepper
½ cup kosher salt
½ cup brown sugar
1 quart rendered duck fat

CELERY ROOT SLAW

1 tablespoon whole-grain mustard
2 teaspoons prepared horseradish
⅓ cup mayonnaise
1 teaspoon fresh lemon juice
1 tablespoon Italian parsley,
  coarsely chopped
2 cups celery root, washed, peeled
  and julienned
¾ cup Granny Smith apple, julienned
Kosher salt and fresh ground
  black pepper

Duck Leg Confit with Whole-Grain Mustard-Celery Root Slaw
4 SERVINGS

Preparation of Duck Confit

In a food processor, place the garlic, shallot, thyme, rosemary, black pepper, kosher salt, and brown sugar. Start the processor by pulsing at first, and then run one additional minute to incorporate all the ingredients.

Place one-third of this mixture in the bottom of a glass baking dish. Place the duck legs on top, and then completely cover the legs with the remainder of the mixture. Cover with plastic wrap and refrigerate overnight.

After 24 hours, remove the duck legs from the mixture. Rinse them briefly under cold water to remove any of the remaining curing mixture. Pat them dry and set aside.

Melt the rendered duck fat in a deep oven safe dish (8-inches square by 4-inches deep). Once the duck fat is liquefied, carefully submerge the duck legs in the duck fat. Place the dish in 275° oven and cook until the duck is very tender, approximately 2½ hours. When finished, the duck can be refrigerated in its own fat for up to a couple of weeks.

Preparation of Mustard-Celery Root Slaw

Place the whole-grain mustard, horseradish, mayonnaise, and lemon juice into a medium-sized mixing bowl and whisk together. Add the julienned celery root, apples, and chopped parsley. Toss together by hand until all the ingredients are incorporated. Adjust seasoning with salt and pepper. Refrigerate until ready to serve.

To Assemble and Plate

When ready to serve the confit, remove the duck legs from the excess fat. Heat a tablespoon or two of the rendered fat in a cast iron skillet over moderate heat. Place the duck legs in the hot fat, skin side down. Cook until nicely browned, then flip over and brown the other side. When the legs are evenly browned and warmed through, they are ready to serve. The leftover duck fat can be strained, refrigerated and reused at a later date.

Place one serving of slaw on plate. Decoratively place one duck leg on top of slaw.

The earthiness of the duck confit and celery root provide a great foundation for pairing it with Chloe Creek Pinot Noir. The crisp sweet and sour taste of the Granny Smith apple adds a fruity note which helps to balance the dish, while the mustard and horseradish round out the dish with a little 'zing'.

1 tablespoon olive oil

1 cup soy sauce

Freshly ground white pepper

6 cups hon dashi broth with bonito *

1 teaspoon chopped garlic

2 cups brown and black rice *

1 tablespoon butter

1 tablespoon Parmesan

4 pounds lobster tail

4 pieces of wild shrimp

3 pieces of grilled asparagus

2 tablespoons of sake *

*Available at Asian food stores

Seafood Risotto

(Wild Sea Shrimp and Lobster, Brown and Black Risotto)
2 SERVINGS

Preparation

Heat olive oil in a large sauté pan over medium heat. Add the soy sauce and white pepper and stir. To the pan add hon dashi broth and bring the mixture to a boil. Reduce the heat to medium and simmer for 6 minutes. Add the brown and black rice and simmer for 12 minutes, stirring constantly. Add in the butter and Parmesan cheese, simmering again for 2 minutes and stirring constantly.

Clean and trim the wild shrimp and lobster tail. Season the shrimp and lobster tail with soy sauce and pepper. Pan-grill shrimp and lobster tail for 2 minutes and add sake. Remove from the heat.

To Assemble and Plate

Spoon the brown and black risotto in the center of each shallow bowl. Garnish with shrimp, lobster and grilled asparagus.

The earthly flavors exhibited by the risotto and the light textures in the fish pair well with the delicacy you find in Pinot Noir.

Strawberry-Thyme Glazed Hudson Valley Duck Breast over Basil Tossed Rice Noodles with Baby Patty Pan Squash
4 SERVINGS

STRAWBERRY-THYME GLAZE
1 shallot, minced
1 clove garlic, minced
¼ ounce fresh thyme
2 cups fresh or frozen strawberries
1 cup Chloe Creek Pinot Noir
2 cups water
1 cup sugar

BASIL TOSSED RICE NOODLES
12 ounces of rice noodles
½ cup of fresh basil, chopped
1 ounce olive oil
Salt and pepper

BABY PATTY PAN SQUASH
8 ounces baby patty pan squash,
 cut in halves
1 ounce unsalted butter
Salt and pepper

Preparation of Strawberry-Thyme Glaze
Sauté shallot, garlic, thyme and strawberries in pan over medium-high heat. Add Pinot Noir and bring to a hard boil.

Reduce heat to simmer, adding water and sugar. Reduce this mixture until it coats the back of a spoon. Season glaze with salt and black pepper.

Preparation of the Noodles
Bring water to a boil for the rice noodles and cook according to package.

Strain noodles and chill under cold running water. In a mixing bowl, toss noodles with oil and basil. Season with salt and pepper.

Preparation of the Squash
Melt butter in a sauté pan and add squash, cooking until tender. Season squash with salt and pepper.

To Assemble and Plate
Be sure duck breasts are cleaned of silver skin. Make 3 little slits in the fat on top of breast as well. Sear the duck breast fat side down on medium heat in a cast iron pan until fat is crispy. Flip breasts and cook an additional 5 minutes. Remove and let rest.

Put 4 ounces of rice noodles in a serving bowl and place a sliced duck breast fanned out around the noodles. Place 2 ounces of the patty pan squash on one side of the dish and then glaze the duck with the sauce.

The inspiration to pair this dish with Pinot Noir was the earthy flavors of local herbs and vegetables, mixed with the unique duck flavor of local Hudson Valley duck breast, which is lacquered with strawberries to set off and balance the dish and most Pinot Noirs.

4 cups mussels, cleaned

SAFFRON-TOMATO BROTH

2 teaspoons olive oil

½ cup garlic, minced

1 teaspoon saffron

6 cups diced tomatoes

1 cup dry white wine

1 tablespoon fresh lemon juice

¼ teaspoon crushed red pepper

FOR GARNISH

2 tablespoons fresh flat-leaf
 parsley, chopped

2 tablespoons fresh basil, chopped

Discard any mussels that do not close when alive or do not open when cooked.

Prince Edward Island Mussels in a Saffron-Tomato Broth

3 TO 4 SERVINGS

Preparation

Heat olive oil in a large pot over medium heat. Add garlic and saffron to pot and sweat until tender. Add tomatoes and sauté until tender. Then add wine, lemon juice and pepper, bringing to a boil. Reduce heat and simmer 25 minutes, or until reduced by three-quarters. Add mussels and simmer until all mussels open, about 5 minutes.

To Assemble and Plate

Portion a serving into bowl and finish with parsley and basil.

The simplicity of this dish is what makes it so attractive. The balance of fresh local ingredients, imported saffron and Prince Edward Island mussels creates a perfect flavor profile.

Empire Steak

(Barrel Cut NY Strip Steak with Cipollini and Shiitake Mushroom Ragout)
1 SERVING

DRY RUB

2 teaspoons mixed
   peppercorns, ground
2 teaspoons kosher salt
1 teaspoon garlic powder
1 teaspoon onion powder
One 10-ounce New York sirloin steak,
   barrel cut **
1 tablespoon vegetable oil

RAGOUT

1 tablespoon whole butter
½ tablespoon garlic, minced
½ tablespoon shallots, minced
3 large shitake mushrooms, sliced
¼ cup Chloe Creek Pinot Noir
¼ cup brown beef stock
2 cipollini onions, quartered
 and roasted
1 sprig fresh rosemary, finely chopped
1 sprig fresh thyme, finely chopped
Salt and pepper

** Barrel cut - The steak is cut from
   a whole New York sirloin which is
   first cut vertically in half, netting
   two "tenderloin-like" loins; from
   each of those a nice, 3½-inch-thick
   cut of sirloin is possible at a lean
   weight of 10-ounces. Your finished
   fabrication should resemble
   a "barrel" looking filet as opposed
   to the traditional long and thin
   New York strip.

Preparation

Combine pepper, salt, garlic and onion to make dry rub. Generously coat all sides of the steak with rub and brush with oil.

Heat sauté pan over high heat until ready to sear the meat. Place steak in pan and let cook for 4 minutes on each side. Remove steak from pan and let rest.

Reduce to medium-high heat and add whole butter to same pan. Add garlic, shallots and shiitakes. Stir quickly for one minute, and do not allow garlic to burn. Deglaze pan with Pinot Noir, reduce by half. Add beef stock and reduce again by half. Add cipollini onions and fresh herbs. Stir and season with salt and pepper.

To Assemble and Plate

Place steak on hot dinner plate and serve ragout across the top. Best to pair with a local seasonal starch and vegetable.

The Empire Steak, is a bold new approach to the classic presentation of "the NY strip," which we saw as a perfect fit to the wine that boasts a similar complexity. The 2009 Russian River Valley is in its own way a new take on "the classic Pinot Noir."

The choice flavors to match this steak are easily paired with a wine rich in berry sweetness and earthy oak tones. The cipollini onions take on their own great natural sweetness when roasted and the shiitake mushroom is easily a great earthy addition to any steak entrée. The addition of peppercorns and garlic to the steak and garden fresh thyme and rosemary to the ragout continue to play well off of the naturally sweet and savory palate, that which the wine will help to explore.

Much like its pairing vineyard, the inspiration behind this dish was to build a "new plate with and old concept." We think we've done that here.

Grilled Rib-Eye Steak with Garlicky Broccoli Rabe and Tomato-Pepper Jam
4 SERVINGS

BROCCOLI RABE
2 bunches broccoli rabe

4 cloves garlic, slivered

1 tablespoon crushed red pepper

¼ cup olive oil, divided

Kosher salt

Black pepper

TOMATO-PEPPER JAM
2 tablespoons vegetable oil

1 red pepper, halved with stems
  and seeds removed and diced

¼ cup white onion, small diced

1 tablespoon garlic, minced

1 quart tomato strips*

¼ cup banana peppers, chopped

1 cherry pepper, seeds and stem
  removed and chopped

¼ cup sugar

¼ cup white balsamic vinegar

½ teaspoon salt

STEAKS
Four 14- to 16-ounce rib-eye steaks

Kosher salt

Cracked pepper

Olive oil

* Available at specialty and
  gourmet food stores

Preparation of Broccoli Rabe
Prepare a large ice bath.

In a large sauce pot, bring 1 gallon of water to a rolling boil and then add ¼ cup kosher salt. Trim and discard ¼-inch of the end of the broccoli rabe stems. Place reserved broccoli rabe in salted water. Cook until the stems collapse when squeezed. Remove from water and place in ice bath to chill. When completely cooled, remove from ice bath and drain well. Lightly squeeze as much excess moisture as possible from broccoli rabe and pat dry with paper towels.

Heat half of the olive oil in a large sauté pan over high heat. When oil is hot and shimmering, add broccoli rabe. Sauté quickly and add garlic, crushed pepper and remaining olive oil.

When garlic is lightly browned and broccoli rabe is hot throughout, season with salt and pepper. Remove from pan and place on a platter.

Preparation of Tomato Pepper Jam
In a medium sauté pan, heat oil over medium-high heat. Sauté onions, red pepper, garlic until lightly browned and soft. Add remaining ingredients and turn heat to low. Reduce while stirring frequently until a jam-like consistency is reached.

To Assemble and Plate
Rub steaks with olive oil and season liberally with salt and pepper. Grill until desired temperature is reached. Set aside to redistribute juices. Serve with Tomato-Pepper Jam on top of steak and a side of broccoli rabe.

The sweet and tart tomato jam in this dish pairs very well with the rich rib eye steak and the pungent and garlicky broccoli rabe. The jam can be paired with almost any other type of meat or fish and goes very well with the jammy, sun ripened fruit flavor notes of Pinot Noir.

FISH

Four 6- to 7-ounce swordfish chops
  or swordfish steaks
Salt and pepper
Olive oil

CELERIAC MOUSSELINE

1 celery root
2 ounces unsweetened
  whipped cream
Salt
Ground fennel
White pepper

BRAISED LEEKS

1 bunch baby leeks
  or scallions, green stalk removed
1 cup chicken broth
3 sprigs thyme
1 clove garlic
Salt and pepper

BLACK PEPPER-PINOT NOIR JUS

2 cups Chloe Creek Pinot Noir
2 tablespoons sugar
1 bulb shallot, minced
1 clove garlic
1 cup clam Juice
1 cup chicken broth
1/2 teaspoon cracked black pepper
1/4 cup unsalted butter

GARNISH

2 icicle radish or daikon*
Olive oil
Fleur de Sel
Ground fennel seed
Few pinches radish micro greens
2 icicle radish or daikon*

*Available at specialty and
  gourmet food stores

*My childhood on the coast of Maine
when I always requested swordfish
on my birthday..... There was
always something missing; I now
know it was the Pinot Noir.*

Grilled Georges Bank Swordfish Chop with Celeriac Mousseline, Braised Baby Leeks and Black Pepper-Pinot Noir Jus
4 SERVINGS

Preparation of Swordfish Chops

Have your fishmonger special order chops or 6-to 7-ounce block-cut swordfish, skin off, bloodline removed. Season chops with salt and cracked black pepper. Drizzle with olive oil and refrigerate.

Preparation of Celeriac Mousseline

Peel 1 large celery root and cut into large dice. Place celery root in salted water and simmer until tender. Drain and puree through a food mill or ricer. Keep warm.

Whip the cream until light and fluffy (soft peak). Fold whipped cream into celery root puree in thirds until light and fluffy. Season to taste with ground fennel, white pepper and salt. Reserve and keep warm.

Preparation of Braised Baby Leeks

In a heavy-bottomed pot, place baby leeks or scallion bulbs into chicken broth. Add thyme and garlic to the leeks. Season with salt and pepper. Lightly simmer until leeks are tender. Remove leeks and cool; reserve some liquid to reheat leeks when ready to plate.

Preparation of Black Pepper-Pinot Noir Jus

In a heavy-bottomed pan lightly caramelize sugar. Deglaze pan with Pinot Noir and reduce by a one-third or until alcohol has cooked out. Add shallot, garlic, chicken broth and clam juice. Reduce sauce until it coats the back of a spoon.

Season with salt and generously with cracked black pepper for a pronounced flavor. Slowly whisk in unsalted butter. Reserve and keep warm.

To Assemble and Plate

Preheat grill on medium to medium-high heat. Brush and lightly oil grill racks. Remove fish from refrigerator. Place on grill and cook with lid open until done, roughly 4 minutes per side.

Spoon a generous amount of Celeriac Mousseline on the left side of each plate, dragging back of spoon through puree to the right side of the plate to make a swoosh. Line up 3 or 4 baby leek bulbs in center of plate to form a small pile of sticks. Place swordfish on top of leeks.

Drizzle Black Pepper-Pinot Noir Jus over fish and around plate. Shave icicle radish on a mandoline over the top of fish and finish with micro greens and fleur de sel.

LOBSTER FILLING

5 ounces lobster meat
  (whole female lobster, hard shell
  only and reserve shells)
½ teaspoon unsalted butter
1 cup of leeks, washed and julienned
  into 1-inch lengths
½ cup chanterelle mushrooms
½ cup dry white wine
Salt and pepper
2 tablespoons Lobster Sauce
  (recipe follows)

LOBSTER SAUCE

Reserved shells – not antennae
1 teaspoon unsalted butter
½ cup celery, roughly chopped
½ cup carrots, roughly chopped
½ cup onions, roughly chopped
1 cup of tomatoes, very ripe and
  roughly chopped
1 cup dry white wine
1 teaspoon fresh tarragon
1 cup heavy cream
3 ounces of good brandy or cognac
1 teaspoon lobster roe
1 teaspoon kosher salt
½ teaspoon fresh ground
  black pepper
1 teaspoon unsalted butter

PUFF PASTRY BOX

One 4-by-4-inch piece of puff pastry
1 whole egg

CORN SAUCE

1 ear fresh local corn, kernels
  removed and reserved
2 tablespoons shallots, minced
½ teaspoon butter
¼ cup dry white wine
1½ cups chicken stock
Salt and pepper

ASPARAGUS BUNDLES

4 of each green and white asparagus
Strips of leek, blanched green part

Lobster Louis the Thirteenth
1 SERVING

Preparation of Filling

Cook, cool and de-shell lobster. Slice tail into medallions. In a small skillet add ½ teaspoon of butter, leeks, and chanterelle mushrooms. Sauté until leeks are translucent. Add ½ cup of white wine and reduce by half. Add 2 tablespoons of the lobster sauce and all lobster meat. Cook on low for 2 minutes. Add salt and pepper to taste.

Preparation of Lobster Sauce

In large skillet, heat butter and add all celery, carrots, onions, tomatoes and crushed lobster shells. Start to lightly caramelize. Once a nice dark red color has formed, add 1 cup dry white wine and reduce by half. Add heavy cream and cognac to the skillet, and cook down until slightly thickened. Add salt and pepper to taste. Strain sauce through fine mesh. Add all liquid to small sauté pan and reduce by half. Add 1 teaspoon of butter, tarragon and finish with cooked lobster roe.

Preparation of Puff Pastry

Cut out 2-by-3-inch rectangular box from puff pastry. Then cut ¼-inch strips for a border around the edge of the box. Brush with egg wash. Bake on flat sheet in a 400° oven for 4 minutes. Let cool and cut center out.

Preparation of Corn Sauce

In a small skillet, add chopped shallots, corn kernels and ½ teaspoon butter. Cook vegetables slowly for 3 minutes. Add wine and chicken stock. Simmer until most of liquid has evaporated. Puree in blender and strain through fine mesh. Add salt and pepper to taste.

Preparation of Asparagus Bundles

Cut and discard the bottom 3 -inches of the stalks. Peel bottom halves of asparagus. Blanch in boiling water for 2 minutes and then shock in ice water. Tie each bundle (3 white and 3 green) with a small strip of blanched green leek. Reheat bundles in butter and a splash of water.

To Assemble and Plate

Place cooked puff pastry in center of a large plate. Fill center with lobster filling. Add claw meat to right and left front of dish. Add asparagus to right and left center of dish. Spoon dots of corn sauce on outside edge. Drizzle lobster sauce around center of dish. Garnish with lobster antennae.

Nothing goes together better than just-picked August corn and hard shell cold-water lobster. Enjoy this entree without the fuss of shells. Indulge on lobster chunks, puff pastry, golden chanterelles, and a rich lobster-cognac sauce. Bon appetite!

ROULADE

Four 8-ounce salmon fillets
  (longer is better)
6 ounces goat cheese
4 long slices of prosciutto
1 cup leeks, thinly sliced
1 tablespoon olive oil
½ cup white wine
Salt and pepper

BEURRE ROUGE SAUCE

1 cup Chloe Creek Pinot Noir
1 large shallot, minced
½ lemon, juiced
½ cup heavy cream
2 tablespoons butter
Salt and pepper

Salmon Roulade with Pinot Beurre Rouge
4 SERVINGS

Preparation of Roulade

Slice salmon lengthwise so you have a total of 8 long pieces. Turn them on their sides and roll, making a circle and leaving a hole in the center. Split each piece of prosciutto and wrap around outside of salmon to hold them together. Fill the center of the salmon with approximately ¾ ounce of goat cheese. Grease baking pan with olive oil and place salmon on it. Lightly season salmon with salt and pepper, and then top salmon with thinly sliced leeks. To the pan, add white wine and cook in a 450° oven for 10 to 12 minutes or until desired doneness.

Preparation of Beurre Rouge Sauce

In a sauce pan, add Pinot Noir, shallot and lemon juice. Bring to a simmer and reduce by half. Add heavy cream and continue to reduce by almost half. Slowly add butter a little at a time, using a whisk and stirring constantly. After all the butter is incorporated, season with salt and pepper.

To Assemble and Plate

Place salmon on plate with your favorite starch and vegetable add the Beurre Rouge over fish.

I love food to be more than one-dimensional, and with this dish you have a combination of textures and flavors. The firm flesh of the salmon, the creamy goat cheese, the robust flavor of the prosciutto and bitter sweet leeks make a great pairing with a glass of Pinot Noir.

Two 1½- to 2½-pound pheasants,
  cut up
½ cup flour
2 teaspoons salt
½ teaspoon pepper
1 teaspoon fresh thyme, chopped
6 tablespoons butter
2 tablespoons oil
2 cups pearl onions, peeled
2 cups fingerling potatoes, sliced
½ cup fine sherry (Savory & James)
½ cup Chloe Creek Pinot Noir
25 ounces chicken stock
1 teaspoon garlic
1 cup fresh peas, shelled
½ tablespoon fresh thyme, chopped
1 cup heavy cream
3 tablespoons fresh parsley, chopped
  and divided
Salt and pepper

Pheasant Fricassee
4 SERVINGS

Preparation of Pheasant

Combine the flour with the salt, pepper, and thyme. Dredge the pheasant pieces in the seasoned flour. Heat a heavy-bottom skillet and add butter and 2 tablespoons oil. Brown the pheasant, making sure to baste the meat often during the process. Once all pieces are browned, remove and reserve.

Add the onions and potatoes to the skillet. Deglaze with the sherry and reduce until dry. Add the red wine and reduce by half. To this mixture, add the garlic and chicken stock. Put pheasant back into skillet and place into a preheated 350° oven. Bake for 35 to 40 minutes, basting often.

Remove the pheasant from the skillet and reserve. In the same skillet over high heat, reduce the cooking liquid by half. Add the peas, thyme and cream. Reduce by half. Add 2 tablespoons of parsley and adjust salt and pepper. Add the pheasant back in, cooking over medium heat for 3 to 5 minutes.

To Assemble and Plate

Place the vegetable mixture in a shallow bowl. Place a breast and leg on top of vegetables. Spoon the sauce over pheasant and vegetables and sprinkle with remaining parsley.

My motto at Maestro's is to put love on the plate. This dish is a great example of that, and the earthiness of the sherry used in the recipe really pops when paired with Pinot Noir.

BBQ Lamb Ribs, Humboldt Fog Ravioli, Matsutake Mushrooms, English Peas and Smoked Red Beets
4 SERVINGS

Note: need smoker for beets

RIBS

3 pounds lamb Denver ribs

2 tablespoons canola oil

1 large onion, diced

½ cup carrots, diced small

½ cup celery, diced small

2 teaspoons garlic, minced

1 cup red wine

1 pint lamb stock or water

Salt and pepper

BBQ SAUCE

1 cup 677 steak sauce**

1 cup ketchup

½ teaspoon liquid smoke

RAVIOLI

48 gyoza skins*

12 ounces Humboldt fog cheese*

24 flat-leaf parsley leaves

1 egg, beaten

¼ cup warm melted butter

SMOKED RED BEETS

8 baby red beets

½ cup of hickory chips for smoking

MATSUTAKE MUSHROOMS

8 medium matsutake mushrooms
 cut in half

1 teaspoon shallots, minced

1 tablespoon butter

ENGLISH PEAS

½ cup fresh shucked English peas

1 tablespoon butter

1 teaspoon white truffle oil

*Available at specialty and
 gourmet food stores

**Available at 677 Prime

I love classic flavor combinations using seasonal ingredients to create a dish that's familiar but feels exciting and new.

Preparation of Ribs

Heat oil in a large sauté pan and sear ribs until golden. Remove ribs from pan. To the pan add onions, carrots, celery and garlic, cooking until caramelized. Add wine to the vegetables and cook for 2 minutes add stock and bring to a boil.

Place ribs in a large roasting pan and pour liquid over them. Cover tightly with plastic and foil and bake in a 215° oven for 5 hours. When done, remove from heat and cool. Puree sauce from pan with an immersion blender and strain. Season the sauce with salt and pepper and set aside until ready to serve.

Preparation of BBQ Sauce

Combine steak sauce, ketchup and liquid smoke. Chill and reserve for the ravioli.

Preparation of Ravioli

Lay out 24 gyoza skins and place ¼-ounce of cheese in each center. Top the cheese with a parsley leaf and brush edges of gyoza skins with egg. Top with another gyoza skin and press edges to seal. Use a round cutter to cut the ravioli down to size and place on an oiled pan a set aside until ready to cook.

Preparation of Smoked Red Beets

Simmer baby beets with skins on in salted water until tender. Remove from water and let cool slightly. Rub skins off with a towel and place beets in a smoker containing hickory chips. Smoke over medium heat for 10 minutes. Remove from smoker and cut into quarters. Keep beets in warm butter until ready to serve.

Preparation of Matsutake Mushrooms

Heat butter and cook mushrooms until well browned. Add shallots to the mushrooms and cook for 2 minutes. Season with salt and pepper. Set aside until ready to serve, keep warm.

Preparation of English Peas

Heat peas and butter over low heat until softened. Add truffle oil and salt. Reserve until ready to serve.

To Assemble and Plate

Boil water for ravioli and preheat oven to 350°. Heat and spoon refined sauce onto serving plate. Toss ribs in BBQ Sauce and heat ribs in oven.

Drop ravioli in boiling salted water and cook for 2 minutes. Remove ravioli from water and toss in a bowl with olive oil, salt and pepper. Place ravioli onto serving plate and place hot ribs onto the refined braising sauce. Spoon the warm beets, mushrooms and peas onto the plate in a decorative layout. Spoon extra BBQ Sauce and braising sauce around the plate. Garnish with fine herbs or micro greens.

GREEN PASTA
10 leaves of basil
20 leaves baby spinach
2 tablespoons extra-virgin olive oil
1½ cups unbleached flour
2 eggs

PEA FILLING
1 pound frozen or fresh peas
10 fresh mint leaves
3 tablespoons fresh ricotta
1 tablespoon fresh Parmesan
Salt and black pepper

CARROTS
24 baby carrots
Salt and pepper
Unsalted butter

PEARL ONIONS
4 ounces peeled pearl onions
1 cup balsamic vinegar
Salt and black pepper
1 tablespoon brown sugar

ROASTED RACK OF LAMB
Two 8-bone racks of lamb,
 frenched
Kosher or sea salt and freshly
 ground black pepper
Canola oil

The inspiration for my lamb dish springs from stories that my wife told me about her childhood and her Italian grandmother. When spring would begin, her grandmother would prepare feasts for her large family; traditionally lamb would be a centerpiece and would always be accompanied by a minted spring pea casserole. Recalling her stories about these family meals, it wasn't too much of a leap to modify the casserole into minted pea ravioli and serve them with a rack of lamb.

Roasted Lamb Rack with Minted Spring Pea Ravioli, Roasted Baby Carrots and Balsamic Pearl Onions
8 SERVINGS

Preparation of Pasta
In a blender, puree the spinach and basil leaves with the oil. Pour the flour on a work surface, shape it into a mound and make well in the center. Break the eggs into the well and whisk gently with a fork. Blend the basil puree into the eggs until completely incorporated. Draw a little flour into the eggs, slowly continue combining until the eggs are thick and don't run. Work the flour into the egg mixture with your hands until smooth. Knead the dough about 8 minutes or until the pasta is smooth. Cover and set pasta aside.

Preparation of Pea Filling
If using fresh peas, cook until tender but still bright green. If using frozen peas, boil briefly to ensure completely thawed. Puree the peas and mint. Strain pulp through a fine mesh strainer leaving behind the skins. Blend in the ricotta and Parmesan and season to taste.

Preparation of Ravioli
Roll the pasta through your pasta machine according to manufactures suggestions. Lay out a single sheet and dot in equal measured distance the pea filling. Lightly brush water on the bottom sheet, around the pea filling, and place another top pasta sheet and press firmly around the fillings. Using a pasta wheel cut even squares of ravioli. Roll out 24 ravioli. In a pot of gently boiling water drop in ravioli and cook until tender. Remove and reserve.

Preparation of Carrot Sauce
Place butter in a sauté pan on medium heat and toss in the carrots with seasonings. Deglaze with a little water and cook gentle until the carrots are tender.

Preparation of Pearl Onions
Preheat the oven to 325°. Toss onions with balsamic, brown sugar and seasonings. Roast covered for 30 to 40 minutes until tender.

Preparation of Lamb Racks
Preheat oven to 450°. Season each rack on all sides with salt and pepper. In a large sauté pan heat a little canola oil on medium heat. Place the racks fat side down and sear until golden brown. Drain fat from the pan and place in the oven. Roast the racks, fat side down for 25 to 35 minutes, until the temperature in the center of the rack reads 128° to 130°. Remove from the oven and allow the meat to rest for about 20 minutes.

To Assemble and Plate
Place three ravioli, two onions and three carrots on each plate. Carve each rack into four 2-bone chops and place on each plate.

2 tablespoons olive oil for sauté

Three 16/20 count shrimp

Four 20/30 count sea scallops

2 calamari with tentacles
 (cleaned and cut into rings)

4 littleneck clams

8 mussels

½ teaspoon garlic, chopped

¼ cup tomato, chopped

¼ cup leeks, julienne cut

¼ cup roasted red peppers

¼ cup calamata olives
 (pitted and halved)

¼ cup basil, cut chiffonade

¼ cup white wine

¼ cup fish stock

½ cup virgin olive oil

Salt and pepper to taste

1 pound spinach linguine

1 whole sprig of basil

Discard any clams that do not close when alive or do not open when cooked.

LINGUINE ALL' ADRIATICA
2 SERVINGS

Preparation

Pan-sear shrimp and scallops in 1 tablespoon of olive oil and set aside.

Add remaining tablespoon of olive oil to the hot pan and sauté the calamari, clams and mussels until the clams start to open. Add chopped garlic to the sauté, but do not brown. Add tomatoes, leeks, roasted red pepper, calamata olives and basil and sauté until hot. Deglaze pan with white wine and reduce by half. Add fish stock, virgin olive oil, salt and pepper. Remove clams from shells. Discard shells. Add seared shrimp and scallops to the pan and sauté until hot; season to taste.

To Assemble and Plate

Cook linguine according to directions. Drain pasta. Serve the seafood mixture over spinach linguine and garnish with basil.

The use of native shellfish, rich olive oil and fresh herbs is Northern Italian health-conscious cuisine at its best.

1 bulb of fennel, fronds removed
  and reserved
Olive oil
Salt and pepper
8 to 12 fingerling potatoes
Two 7- to 8-ounce wild striped bass
  fillets (prefer two thick pieces cut
  from a larger fish)
1½ to 2 cups sliced mushrooms,
  oyster, shiitake and domestic
4 to 6 cipollini onions, peeled
  and quartered
2 to 3 cloves garlic, sliced
1 heirloom or beefsteak tomato,
  cored and large diced
6 to 8 ounces Chloe Creek Pinot Noir
8 ounces fish or vegetable stock

Wild Striped Bass Braised with Red Wine, Mushrooms and Heirloom Tomatoes, Roasted Fennel and Fingerling Potatoes

2 SERVINGS

Preparation

Pat fish dry, making sure all scales are removed. Score the skin with the tip of a sharp knife in a cross hatch pattern, a half inch apart. Do not cut too deeply into the flesh. Just prior to cooking, season the fish with sea salt and black pepper.

Remove the fennel fronds (reserve fronds for garnish) and stems. Quarter the bulb top to bottom and remove the core, leaving just enough of the core to hold the fennel together. Roast the fennel in an oven dish with olive oil, salt, pepper and thyme at 350° for 25 to 30 minutes or until tender, turning the pieces over halfway through. This can be done ahead of time and fennel can be reheated in the oven just prior to plating. Rinse and halve fingerlings lengthwise, reserve in cold water. Simmer potatoes in salted water for approximately 20 minutes.

Heat a 10 or 12-inch skillet over medium-high heat. Oil the pan, making sure it doesn't smoke, and place the bass in the pan skin side down. Cook skin side for 2 to 3 minutes and then turn over and cook for 2 more minutes. Remove fish from the pan.

Bring the pan back up to temperature and add more oil if necessary. Add sliced mushrooms and sauté briefly 1 to 2 minutes. Add cipollini onions and cook another two minutes. Add garlic and cook for a minute, being careful not to brown. Add tomato, toss with other vegetables briefly and then deglaze with red wine. Reduce wine by one-third and then add stock. Return liquid to a simmer and add fish back to pan, skin side up. Cover loosely with parchment paper and cook in oven for 8 to 10 minutes, paying attention not to overcook fish. Remove the fish from the pan when cooked, firm and flakey, and reduce liquid further if necessary. Liquid should be intense and flavorful, not watery. Season with salt and pepper.

To Assemble and Plate

Place some fingerlings in the center of a large bowl. Place fish on the potatoes (removing skin is optional). Spoon the sauce with mushrooms and tomatoes around the fish. Place half of the roasted fennel to the side of the fish and garnish with the fresh fennel fronds.

This dish goes against the old "no red wine with fish" rule and is one of my favorites from early summer. The big fresh flavors of mushrooms, fennel, and tomatoes marry well with Pinot Noir and still let the delicate flavor of the bass through.

Marinated Lucki 7 Pork Chop with Savory Apple-Bacon Waffle, Roasted Parsnips and Chutney Jus
4 SERVINGS

4 pork chops, marinated overnight in Miss Sydney's Original Marinade*

PARSNIPS
2 pounds parsnips, julienned
½ cup oil
Salt and pepper

CHUTNEY JUS
½ cup Miss Sydney's Indu's Chutney *
½ cup water

WAFFLES
4 slices bacon, finely diced
1 small white onion, finely diced
1 apple, finely diced
2 teaspoons chicken base
2 tablespoons maple syrup
2 tablespoons dark rum
1 cup Bisquick
1 cup milk
1 egg

*Available at specialty and gourmet food stores or online at Miss Sydney's

Preparation
Preheat oven to 400° and plug in a waffle iron.

Spread the julienned parsnips on a baking sheet. Coat the parsnips evenly with oil, salt and pepper. Bake parsnips in oven for 45 minutes to 1 hour, or until caramelized.

While parsnips roast, make the Chutney Jus by combining Indu's Chutney and water and set aside.

In a large nonstick pan, caramelize the bacon for 5 to 7 minutes or until crispy. Add the onions and cook until soft and caramelized. Add the apples, chicken base, maple syrup and cook for an additional 2 to 3 minutes. Add the rum and cook for about 1 to 2 minutes or until reduced. Let mixture cool.

Turn parsnips over on the pan in the oven and continue baking until fully done. While parsnips roast, grill marinated pork chops until done, about 5 minutes per side or 155°.

In the meantime, mix Bisquick, milk and egg together until smooth. Mix the cooled apple mixture into the waffle batter until completely blended. Make the waffles and set aside.

To Assemble and Plate
Place a pork chop on serving plate. Then place the waffle on top of pork chop. Add roasted parsnips on waffle and pour Chutney Jus over top.

Pinot and pork is for the cook what canvas is for the painter – imagination and creativity at its finest. We also try to use New York state products as much as possible.

SALMON

10 sprigs fresh thyme

4 fresh bay leaves

1 large sprig fresh rosemary

2 cloves garlic, peeled and
  lightly crushed

1 tablespoon lemon zest

3 cups regular olive oil or more
  to cover fish

Four 5- to 6-ounce center-cut salmon
  fillets, char or steelhead trout fillets
  at room temperature

Salt and black pepper

PINOT NOIR SAUCE

1 cup dry red wine

2 bay leaves

1 teaspoon fresh thyme leaves

1 shallot, minced

1 clove garlic, smashed

¼ cup carrot, diced small

1 cup chicken or vegetable stock

¼ cup butter, softened

Salt and black pepper

Olive Oil-Poached Salmon with Pinot Noir Sauce
4 SERVINGS

Preparation of Salmon

Combine thyme, bay leaves, rosemary, garlic and lemon zest and oil in a pot just wide enough to hold fish in a single layer without touching. When fish is added, oil should cover it, so it is better to use more oil than not enough. Season fish on both sides with salt and pepper.

Fit skillet with a deep-frying thermometer and heat oil to 160° over medium-low heat. Reduce heat and monitor temperature, adjusting until temperature is a stable 160° (with small bubbles occasionally rising to surface).

When temperature is stable, add fish. Oil temperature will drop, so raise heat slightly (never above medium-low) until it reaches 160° again; then reduce.

Cook fish 13 to 15 minutes, until top is completely opaque and flakes easily with a fork.

Preparation of Pinot Noir Sauce

Put the wine, herbs and vegetables in a small, heavy pot. Bring to a boil and reduce by half. Add the stock and reduce by half again, leaving you with a scant ½ cup of rich reduction. Remove from heat, whisk in the butter; reserve to drizzle over the warm salmon.

To Assemble and Plate

Remove fish to a plate lined with paper towels, let drain. Place on serving platter, sprinkle with herbs and serve immediately drizzled with red wine sauce.

Strain and refrigerate the cooking oil. It can be used for cooking, drizzling on salads and dressing tuna salad.

Salmon is a classic pairing to Pinot Noir; the oily, fleshy fish blends beautifully with and adds to the bright fruit characteristics of young Pinot Noir. The sauce provides another bridge to complement both the wine and salmon.

2 pounds calamari, tubes and
  tentacles, cleaned
¼ cup dry wild mushrooms,
  porcini or forest mix
Water to rehydrate mushrooms
Olive oil as needed
2 medium onion, peeled and diced
1 small carrot, peeled and diced
4 cloves garlic, minced
1 cup cremini mushrooms, quartered
  plus 2 cups sliced
2 tablespoons tomato paste
2 tablespoons balsamic vinegar
1 tablespoon squid ink (optional)*
One 28-ounce can plum tomatoes
1 fresh bay leaf
1 bottle Chloe Creek Pinot Noir
Fresh rosemary
Fresh sage
Fresh parsley
Salt and pepper

*Available at specialty and
  gourmet food stores

Red Wine Braised Calamari with Mushrooms
4 SERVINGS

Preparation

Slice the calamari tubes into 1- inch rings. Leave the tentacles whole.

Put the dry mushrooms into a bowl with enough water to cover and let soak.

In a Dutch oven, heat enough oil to coat the bottom of the pan and add the onions and carrot. Cook over medium heat until the vegetables are beginning to pick up some golden color. Add a small pinch of salt to release the flavors. Add the garlic and cook until lightly golden. Add 2 tablespoons of oil and add the cremini mushrooms, sautéing until the mushrooms are shiny. Next add the tomato paste and stir it in well. Cook for 4 to 5 minutes, stirring regularly to get the whole mass amalgamated and lightly caramelized around the edges.

Remove the mushrooms from the soaking water and squeeze out some liquid (reserve liquid). Add drained mushrooms to the pot. Strain the soaking water and add liquid along with the mushrooms. Season lightly with salt and pepper. Add the balsamic and stir, letting it come to a boil. (if you have the squid ink, add it now) Cook for 3 more minutes. Add the squid, stir to coat. Finally, add the one bay leaf. Squish canned tomatoes through your fingers and add along with wine; bring it all to a boil.

Cook briskly for 3 minutes and then reduce to a low simmer. Cook gently, partially covered for 1 to 1½ hours or until the squid is very tender. Add a small amount of rosemary and sage, and a bit more of parsley and gently stir. Cover completely and let rest for 15 minutes before serving.

To Assemble and Plate

Calamari is best served over pappardelle, a plain risotto or just with a side of garlic roasted potatoes.

The common school of thought is that calamari must be cooked for a very short time to ensure its tenderness, and though this is true, it is only half the story. It is also possible to create a hearty, savory dinner by cooking calamari for hours to make it tender as a soft veal stew. This is a great winter dish as it fills your home with a bewitching aroma while cooking. Be sure to add the ingredients in layers to build complexity in the flavor.

TROUT

1 head of savoy cabbage
  (2 cups shredded)
2 tablespoons extra-virgin
  olive oil, divided
Salt and pepper
½ cup of sherry vinegar
2 cups of white wine
6 to 8 cipollini onions or whole
  small shallots
Four 10-ounce rainbow trout,
  de-boned and filleted
  (head and tail optional)
1 cup micro-beet greens
  (optional garnish)

BEURRE FONDUE

4 medium to large leeks
8 ounces butter (may not use all)

Pan-Seared Rainbow Trout with Braised Savoy Cabbage and Beurre Fondue
4 SERVINGS

Preparation

Preheat oven to 400°.

Shred the savoy cabbage into ¼-inch strips. In a braising pot, over medium heat, add one tablespoon of olive oil. Add the savoy cabbage and sauté until lightly wilted and slightly browned. Season with salt and pepper. Add vinegar and white wine and bring to a strong simmer. Cover the pot and place in a 400° oven for approximately 45 to 60 minutes.

While the cabbage is braising, line a sheet pan with parchment paper and place cipollini onions (skin on) on the sheet pan. Sprinkle with 1 tablespoon of olive oil and put in 400° oven for approximately 30 minutes.

Once the cipollinis have roasted in their skins, allow them to cool. With a pair of scissors, snip the ends of the onions and remove the onions from their skins. Place aside.

Preparation of Beurre Fondue

Dice butter into ½-inch cubes.

Prepare the leek by cleaning off the root end the green tips. Save the green tips for later.

In medium-sized heavy pot, pour enough water to thinly cover the bottom. Bring to a boil. With one hand slowly drop the cubes of butter into pot while continually whisking with the other hand, keeping the butter emulsified in a liquid state. By the end the butter should be light and foamy.

Adjust to a low flame and add the leeks, cooking in the butter for 5 to 6 minutes, or until tender. Whisk intermittently as leeks are cooking. Water from the leeks will thin the butter and infuse it with flavor. When leeks are tender remove from butter and set aside.

Preparation of Pan-Seared Trout

Season fish with salt and pepper.

WITH HEAD AND TAIL ON

On a high flame, sear one side of fish. Baste with 1 or 2 teaspoons of the leek butter. Continue cooking in over for 2 minutes on one side. Flip and cook in oven for another 3 minutes.

WITHOUT HEAD AND TAIL

On a high flame, sear with skin side down. Remove from pan, baste with 1 teaspoon of leek butter on each piece and continue cooking in oven for 4 minutes.

To Assemble and Plate

Pour excess fish oil out of pan. In same pan, quickly sauté the green leek tops that were set aside earlier. Remove and set on napkin to rest for a moment. Season Beurre Fondue with salt to taste. Whisk until frothy again.

Arrange about two tablespoons of braised savoy cabbage onto a plate. Arrange one-half roasted leek on top of the cabbage. Add 2 or 3 roasted cipollini onions. Place freshly seared trout, skin side facing up, on top of the vegetables. Spoon frothy Beurre Fondue over the fish. Garnish with micro-greens and serve.

Devin feels that this preparation will go nicely with Pinot Noir because this dish is flavorful enough with the braised savoy cabbage to be accompanied by a more extracted red wine. Plus, the slight earthy, nutty flavor inherent in the rainbow trout performs perfectly with the subtle earthy tones of the wine. At our dinner table, there is no such thing as the "white wine with fish" rule.

POMMES GRATIN

2 tablespoons butter

1 white onion peeled and sliced thin

4 large potatoes peeled and sliced thin

24 fluid ounces heavy cream

4 sprigs fresh thyme, stemmed
 and chopped

Salt and pepper

TRUFFLE VINAIGRETTE

½ golf ball-sized shallot

1 fluid ounce lemon juice

½ fluid ounces sherry vinegar

1 teaspoon Dijon mustard

1½ fluid ounces truffle juice from
 canned truffle peelings*

½ fluid ounce truffle oil

1 cup canola oil

Salt and pepper

2 tablespoons chopped
 truffle peelings

FOR FINAL DISH

30 scallops

2 ears of fresh corn

3 slices of bacon

2 heads frisée

*Available at specialty and
 gourmet food stores

Truffle Scallop with Pommes Gratin
6 SERVINGS

Preparation of Gratin

Slice onion and cook until translucent in sauce pot with the butter and some salt on medium-low heat. Be careful not to caramelize the onions.

Slice the potatoes into a large pot with the heavy cream, thyme, salt and pepper. Cook over medium heat stirring often until the cream thickens.

Shingle the potatoes in a single layer onto a half-sheet tray or large lasagna dish. Follow with a thin layer of cooked onions, then another layer of potatoes.

Cook covered in a 350° oven for 30 minutes, uncover and cook until golden and knife tender, about 15 minutes.

Cut the finished gratin in half lengthwise then into pieces large enough to fill the inlay of the plate as they will be the canvass for the finished scallop dish.

Preparation of Vinaigrette

Rough chop shallot and combine with lemon juice, sherry vinegar, truffle juice, and Dijon mustard. With a food processor or immersion blender slowly incorporate the oils until emulsified. Add salt and pepper to taste and truffle peelings.

To Assemble and Plate

Remove fresh corn cut from the cob and pan-roast in butter, salt and pepper until caramelized.

Chop and cook bacon. Drain and set aside.

Toss fresh, washed frisée with bacon, pan-roasted corn and truffle vinaigrette. Season large scallops with salt and pepper and cook in nonstick pan with butter, about 2 minutes each side.

Assemble potatoes on plate. Place scallops on top of potatoes and then top with frisée salad. Dress plate with some of the vinaigrette. Top with chopped chives.

Scallops, potatoes, and truffles just seem to sing in harmony for me. Put them together in one dish then throw some bacon into the mix and you have complete heaven. The crisp and delicate, crunchy and creamy textures all play well together in this arena.

1 ounce of dried porcini
  mushrooms (optional)
1 cup boiling water
6- to 8-ounces of salt pork cut
  into ½-inch chunks
4 tablespoons unsalted
  butter, divided
4 pounds trimmed beef chuck,
  cut into 2-inch cubes, patted
  dry with paper towels
Salt
10 or 12 shallots, chopped (2 cups)
2 large, peeled carrots, 1 chopped,
  1 cut into 2-inch chunks
4 or 5 cloves garlic, chopped
2 tablespoons tomato paste
½ cup of brandy, plus
  2 tablespoons to finish dish
1 bottle Chloe Creek Pinot Noir
1 cup or more low-sodium
  beef stock
½ cup chopped fresh parsley
2 bay leaves
2 teaspoons dried thyme
4 whole cloves
1 pound fresh shiitake, cremini
  or button mushrooms
24 pearl onions, fresh or frozen

BEURRE MANIÉ
3 tablespoons flour
1 tablespoon butter

Beef Bourguignon
8 TO 10 SERVINGS

Preparation

Pour 1 cup of boiling water over the dried porcini mushrooms and allow them to rehydrate for 30 minutes. Remove the mushrooms and chop coarsely. Pour the soaking water through a paper towel (to remove any dirt or debris) into a bowl and set aside. In a large sauté pan, pour enough water to cover the bottom by ⅛-inch. Over medium heat, cook the salt pork in the pan until the water evaporates, stirring occasionally. Once the water is gone, reduce the heat to medium-low, and continue to cook the salt pork until much of the fat has rendered out of it. Add a tablespoon of butter and continue to cook the salt pork until the pieces are browned and crispy. Use a slotted spoon to remove the salt pork pieces to a large Dutch oven or other large, thick-bottomed, lidded pot.

Increase the heat to medium-high. Brown the beef in batches; leaving space around each piece of sizzling meat ensures that it browns and does not steam. Don't move the pieces of beef in the pan until each piece has a good sear. Continue by turning beef to get browned on another side. This will take 15 to 25 minutes, depending on how large a sauté pan you have. Once browned, remove the beef from the sauté pan and place in the Dutch oven with the salt pork.

When all the beef has browned, add the shallots, the one chopped carrot, and the rehydrated chopped porcini mushrooms (if using). Stir pan to get up all browned stuck-on bits in the pan. Cook for 2 to 3 minutes, and then add the garlic and the tomato paste. Cook another 2 to 3 minutes stirring frequently.

Add the brandy and stir to combine. Boil down by half, then add the strained mushroom soaking water (if using). Scrape any remaining browned bits off the bottom of the sauté pan and pour the contents of the pan into the Dutch oven.

To the Dutch oven, add the bottle of wine and enough beef stock to almost cover the beef; the beef pieces should be barely poking up out of the liquid. Add the parsley, bay leaves, thyme and cloves. Cover and bring to a bare simmer. After 1 hour, add the second carrot, peeled and cut into chunks of 1- to 2-inches. Continue cooking for another hour or until the beef is tender.

Meanwhile, trim the tough stems off the mushrooms and slice into 2 to 3 large pieces; small mushrooms leave whole. Prepare the pearl onions. Boil them in their skins for 4 to 5 minutes. Drain and submerge in a bowl of ice water. Slice the tips and root ends off the onions and slip off the outer skins.

When the beef is tender, use tongs to remove all the beef and the chunks of carrots; set aside in a bowl. Strain the contents of the Dutch oven through a fine-meshed sieve set over a medium pot. Boil this sauce down, tasting frequently. If it begins to taste too salty, turn off the heat. Otherwise, boil down until you have about 3 cups. Turn off the heat.

Heat a large sauté pan over high heat and add the mushrooms. Dry sauté the mushrooms over high heat, shaking the pan and stirring often, until they release their water, about 4 to 5 minutes. Add the pearl onions and 3 tablespoons butter and toss to combine. Sprinkle salt over the onions and mushrooms. Sauté until the onions begin to brown. Remove from heat.

Blend ingredients for Beurre Manié. Returning to the sauce, reduce the heat to medium and whisk in one-third of the paste; wait for it to incorporate into the sauce, and then add another one-third of the paste, and so on. Do not let this boil, but allow it to simmer very gently for 2 to 3 minutes. Stir in the remaining 2 tablespoons of brandy. Season with salt.

To Assemble and Plate

Coat the beef, carrots, mushrooms and pearl onions with the sauce and serve with potatoes, egg noodles or lots of crusty bread.

This is a classic, well-known traditional French recipe. It is a stew prepared with beef braised in red wine – traditionally red Burgundy.

Double-Cut Stuffed Pork Chop with Cherry-Walnut Stuffing, Sautéed Haricots Verts and Apple-Brandy Glaze
4 SERVINGS

STUFFING
Four 12- to 14-ounce pork chops
  (bone-in)
1 slice of bacon
1 tablespoon chop garlic
4 ounces small diced onions
4 ounces small diced celery
1 tablespoon brandy
Salt and pepper
1 loaf of Italian bread
½ cup chicken stock (for broth)
1 bunch of parsley, chopped
4 ounces walnuts, chopped
1 cup dried cherries

APPLE-BRANDY GLAZE
1 teaspoon garlic, chopped
½ cup brandy
4 ounces apple juice
1 tablespoon cold butter
1 teaspoon chopped parsley

HARICOTS VERTS
8 ounces haricots verts
2 tablespoons butter
1 tablespoon water

Preparation for Stuffing
Preheat oven to 350°. Cut Italian bread into 1-ounce cubes. Bake the bread on sheet pan until lightly golden brown.

Dice bacon and cook until crispy. Add garlic and cook until golden brown.

Add celery and onions and cook until tender. Add one tablespoon of brandy to deglaze the pan. Take bread and mix with sautéed vegetables in bowl. Add chicken stock and mix thoroughly. Add parsley, chopped walnuts and dried cherries; season with salt and pepper. Bake uncovered on baking pan at 375° for 20 minutes. Reserve stuffing for later.

Preparation of Pork Chops
Cut a pocket in the side of each pork chop. Take the cooled stuffing and pack into the pocket. Lightly season pork chop with salt and pepper. In a skillet on medium heat with canola oil, lay pork gently into pan and sear both sides of pork chop. Remove and place on baking sheet and place in oven at 375° for 35 minutes or until internal temperature reaches 160°.

Preparation of Apple-Brandy Glaze
Take pan the pork was seared in and add garlic. Cook down and add brandy (Be careful – the alcohol in the brandy will ignite!). Add apple juice and reduce by half. Remove from heat. Add butter and whisk thoroughly until butter is blended. Add parsley.

Preparation of Haricots Verts
While pork is cooking, sauté haricots verts in small amount of butter and add tablespoon of water to finish.

To Assemble and Plate
Remove pork chop and plate to serve. Place 2 ounces of beans to the side of plate. Generously spoon glaze over chop.

Pork is and has remained a favorite dish of mine for as long as I can remember. The flavor and texture remind me of fall nights with my family growing up. It's a staple in my home and I have my mother to thank for that. It's the perfect way to warm up any household!

1 fryer chicken, split into
  four serving pieces
2 ounces pancetta, diced medium
1 bulb fennel, sliced thin
4 ounces mortadella, diced large
8 ounces chicken stock
8 ounces Chloe Creek Pinot Noir
8 ounces tomato puree
1 bunch mustard greens,
  stems removed
4 eggs, poached soft
Sea salt and fresh ground
  black pepper

SCHENECTADY COUNTY COMMUNITY COLLEGE
CULINARY SCHOOL - CHEF CHRISTOPHER TANNER

Chicken Braised with Mortadella and Mustard Greens
4 SERVINGS

Preparation

Heat a large Dutch oven over medium heat, add pancetta and render until pancetta is crispy. Remove pancetta pieces leaving rendered fat in pan. Season the chicken pieces with salt and pepper to taste. Brown on each side in the Dutch oven until skin is crispy, approximately 4 to 5 minutes per side. Remove from pan and set aside.

Add fennel and sauté until lightly caramelized. Add the mortadella, chicken stock, Pinot Noir, and tomato puree and return the chicken pieces and pancetta to pot. Bring to a light boil, reduce heat to a simmer, cover and allow to cook for 20 to 25 minutes or until chicken is cooked through and tender.

While the chicken is cooking, prepare a small pot with water adding a tablespoon of distilled vinegar per quart of water. Bring the water to barely a simmer, add egg and poach until cooked to a soft stage, reserve cooked egg. Poach 4 eggs in this manner.

Add the mustard greens to the Dutch oven with the chicken. Replace the cover and cook an additional 10 minutes or until greens are tender.

To Assemble and Plate

Split the greens between four bowls, surround with mortadella and fennel pieces pouring broth into the bowls. Top the greens with the chicken pieces and top the chicken with the poached egg and garnish with fennel fronds.

Chicken takes on the flavors of wine so well, enhanced with the unctuous mortadella which is balanced with the bitter and spicy mustard greens. Some might find mustard greens overly bitter, but crack that beautiful poached egg over the greens and the fat will mellow those bitter flavors. It is best to drink the wine that you use in your recipes as the flavors will certainly be enhanced in the dish by drinking the wine with it from which the dish was cooked with.

OVEN ROASTED SHALLOTS
4 large shallots
Olive oil
Salt and pepper

CRUST
½ cup prepared horseradish
½ cup finely chopped walnuts
1½ cups panko bread crumbs
1 tablespoon melted butter
1 tablespoon chopped fresh basil
Pinch salt and pepper
Two 14-ounce veal T-bones

SHALLOT-PINOT NOIR
 DEMI-GLAZE
Oven Roasted Shallots
 (recipe above)
1 cup demi-glaze*
½ cup Chloe Creek Pinot Noir

*Available at specialty and
 gourmet food stores

Horseradish-Encrusted Veal T-Bone with Roasted Shallot-Pinot Noir Demi-Glaze
2 SERVINGS

Preparation
Preheat oven to 350°. Place shallots in a roasting pan and drizzle with olive oil, salt and pepper. Roast until tender, about 25 minutes.

Pan-sear veal T-bone slightly under desired doneness. Mix all ingredients for horseradish crust. Place T-bones on oven safe platter and top with approximately a ½-inch layer layer of the horseradish crust. Place under broiler on bottom shelf until browned.

In separate pan over medium heat, reduce Pinot Noir and roasted shallots by half. Add demi-glaze and bring to a simmer.

To Assemble and Plate
Spread 2 ounces of demi-glaze on each plate and top with T-bone. Chef suggests dressing plate with sides of mashed potatoes kicked-up a notch with prosciutto and some Gorgonzola cheese mixed in. Roasted root vegetables are always a good choice.

This is an extraordinarily tender and delicate cut that takes on a matured contrast when enveloped in a horseradish crust and prepared medium-rare.

CANNELLONI

2 pounds sweetbreads
  (cleaned and soaked overnight
  in milk)

Chicken stock

Sachet of bay leaves, black pepper
  and thyme in cheesecloth

Olive oil as needed for sauté

1 cup flour

Salt and pepper

1 tablespoon shallot, minced

1 teaspoon garlic, minced

¼ cup dry sherry

1 cup demi-glaze or brown sauce *
  (reserve ½ cup)

1 teaspoon fresh thyme, minced

½ lemon, juiced

30 wonton skins

LEMONY GLACAGE WITH
  PARMESAN

4 egg yolks

¼ cup white wine

½ lemon, juiced

Tabasco

1 pound clarified butter

Salt and pepper

¼ cup heavy cream, whipped to
  medium peaks

½ cup Parmesan, grated and divided

GARNISH

2 teaspoons chive, minced

2 teaspoons parsley, minced

*Available at specialty and
  gourmet food stores

*Like a winemaker creating a fine
wine, I wanted to create a dish that
was full of flavor, personality and
brilliance – a dish that would be
worth the indulgence and savored
from the first taste to the last bite.*

SPERRY'S - EXECUTIVE CHEF DALE MILLER

Veal Sweetbread Cannelloni with Lemony Glacage and Parmesan
10 SERVINGS

Preparation of Sweetbreads

Remove sweetbreads from milk. In light chicken stock with herb sachet poach sweetbreads on low simmer (200°) for 20 minutes or until firm.

Remove sweetbreads from broth and cool completely. With a sharp knife, remove remaining fat and membrane from sweet bread. Cut the sweetbreads small 1-by-1-by-½-inch-thick medallions and dredge in flour seasoned with salt and pepper.

Sauté sweetbreads in olive oil until crispy and golden brown. Remove from pan onto a sheet pan. Continue sautéing until all sweetbreads are done. Drain excess oil from pan and add shallots and garlic; sauté slightly taking care not to scorch. Deglaze with Sherry and reduce slightly. Add ½ cup demi-glaze and bring to a simmer.

Reserve 10 sweetbread medallions and cut the remainder into a small dice. Add diced sweetbreads back into pan and stir until coated with sauce. Add thyme and season with salt and pepper to taste. Add a squeeze of fresh lemon juice and remove from heat. Allow mixture to cool completely.

When ready, place 3 wonton skins in a row and place about 1 teaspoon of filling onto each wonton. Brush the far end of the dough with warm water and roll the wonton into a cannelloni shape and place on lightly buttered tray seam down. Repeat 9 more times until all of the cannelloni are all stuffed.

Preparation of Glacage

Set up a double at medium high heat.

Begin to whisk egg yolks over double boiler. Continue to whisk untill light in color and texture. Add white wine, lemon juice and 1 or 2 dashes of Tabasco. Slowly pour in clarified butter until a heavy nappe is achieved. Remove from heat and season to taste. Fold in whipped heavy cream and half the amount of Parmesan.

To Assemble and Plate

Cover the cannelloni with foil and place in a 300° oven, heating 4 to 5 minutes until warmed through.

Place the reserved sweetbread medallions in a pan with the reserved demi-glaze and heat until warmed through.

Place 3 cannelloni each in the center of warmed plates and place about a tablespoon of the glacage over the cannelloni. Flash under a broiler until lightly browned. Place a sweetbread medallion in the center of the cannelloni and sprinkle with a small amount of Parmesan cheese. Drizzle a small amount of the demi-glaze around the cannelloni. Garnish with snipped chives or chopped parsley.

Coriander-Crusted Tuna, Shoyu Pressed Watermelon, Melted Kumquat and Avocado Paint

6 SERVINGS

KUMQUAT SAUCE

½ Spanish onion, diced

2 cloves of garlic

1 pound kumquats, de-stemmed

1 quart orange juice

1 tablespoon olive oil

AVOCADO PAINT SAUCE

2 avocados

3 limes, juiced

1 bunch cilantro

1 ounce olive oil

PRESSED WATERMELON

¼ watermelon, cubed

1 cup shoyu or soy sauce*

TUNA

Six 5-ounce portions Ahi tuna

1 teaspoon whole coriander seeds, ground and roasted

3 ounces extra-virgin olive oil or grapeseed oil

Sea salt

*Available at Asian food stores

Preparation of Kumquat Sauce

Sweat onion with garlic until translucent. Add whole kumquat and simmer with orange juice 30 to 45 minutes. Spin in blender until smooth, adding 1 tablespoon of olive oil.

Preparation of Avocado Paint Sauce

Add flesh of 2 avocados in clean blender, with lime juice and cilantro leaves puree until smooth. Adjust with olive oil for desired texture.

Preparation of Pressed Watermelon

Peel half the watermelon and slice into large 1-by-6-inch flat squares and brush with Shoyu. Cover with parchment and press with sheet pan. Repeat process 3 to 5 times for desired flavor.

Preparation of Tuna

Crust with salt and black pepper and ground coriander. Bring sauté pan to high temperature; add vegetable or grapeseed oil. Sear each side of tuna for 30 seconds. Remove from pan. Slice into 3 round medallions.

To Assemble and Plate

Place 1 dollop each of Avocado Paint Sauce and Kumquat Sauce parallel to each other onto the plate, pulling both sauces across plate with small off-set spatula. Place cubed watermelon on 3 spots of the plate, alternating with slices of tuna, cut into thirds. Dress with olive oil and garnish with sea salt.

The dish will pair well with Pinots because of the balanced sweetness from the kumquat fruit and the acidity and fat from avocado, which should bring out a hint of raspberry and plum in Chloe Creek Vineyards' Pinot Noirs.

Sautéed Atlantic Halibut with Gill Farms Sweet Corn, Toy Box Tomatoes and Leeks
4 TO 6 SERVINGS

FISH

Four or six 3-ounce each
halibut fillets
2 lemons
'Wondra' flour
Salt and pepper
Extra-virgin olive oil or vegetable oil

VEGETABLES

2 ounces olive oil
8 ears of corn, stripped off the cob
2 Belgian leeks, washed, cut in half
lengthwise and sliced into
half-moon pieces
2 pints Toy Box or grape tomatoes,
red and yellow preferred, cut in half
Salt and pepper
Basil sprig for garnish

* OPTIONAL: a crispy potato garnish
made with a Japanese vegetable
slicer; essentially a long potato
"string" that's tied in a half-knot
and fried.

Preparation of the Fish

Lightly sprinkle flour on fillets, season with salt and pepper and place a slice of lemon on each fillet.

Pan-fry fillets lemon side down in oil until lightly brown. Turn over fillets leaving lemon slice intact. Finish cooking in a 400° oven for approximately 5 minutes. Fish should be cooked through.

Remove fillets from oven and keep warm.

Preparation of the Vegetables

In a large sauté pan with olive oil, sauté corn. After a few minutes, add leeks and continue sautéing. Finally add in the tomatoes; season with salt and pepper. It's important to start the corn first, as it takes the longest to cook. Vegetables should be cooked lightly. Don't over cook!

To Assemble and Plate

Place sautéed vegetables in shallow 12-inch pasta bowls. Divide vegetables evenly. Place fillet on top of each pile of sautéed vegetables.

Drizzle with exceptional olive oil, place potato crisp garnish or opal basil sprig garnish on top. Serve.

This recipe couldn't be easier to produce. It beautifully represents the adage "simplicity in the greatest form of sophistication." The success of this dish hinges on the freshness of the ingredients.

Four 10-ounce beef tenderloin steaks

CRAB CAKE
1½ teaspoons unsalted butter
2 tablespoons onion, minced
2 tablespoons celery, minced
1 clove garlic
1¼ pounds crab meat
1 teaspoon Worcestershire
1 teaspoon Dijon mustard
1 teaspoon chopped parsley
1 teaspoon Old Bay
1 teaspoon kosher salt
1 tablespoon fresh lemon juice
2½ cups panko breadcrumbs, divided
1 large egg
Flour
Canola oil

SAUCE HOLLANDAISE
8 egg yolks
1 ounce white wine
8 ounces clarified butter
Salt and white pepper
Cayenne pepper

SAUTÉED MUSHROOMS AND POACHED ASPARAGUS
Olive oil
8 ounces mushrooms, sliced
1 pound fresh asparagus
Salt

Filet Oscar
4 SERVINGS

Preparation of Crab Cake
Sweat onion, celery and garlic in butter until soft and refrigerate.

Combine cooked vegetables, crab meat, Worcestershire, Dijon, parsley, Old Bay, salt, lemon juice and 2 cups of panko. Form cakes. Whisk egg. Dredge crab cake lightly in flour, then egg, then remaining panko. Pan-fry in canola oil until golden. Finish in a 350° oven until warm in center.

Preparation of Hollandaise
Egg yolks and white wine are whisked over a hot water bath until frothy and slightly thickened. Take the sauce off the heat and whisk in butter, slowly, to emulsify. Season the sauce with salt, white pepper, and cayenne pepper to taste.

Preparation of Sautéed Mushrooms
In a medium frying pan, heat olive oil and sauté mushrooms until browned.

Preparation of Asparagus
Snap ends off of asparagus. Steam or poach asparagus in boiling lightly salted water until tender, about 10 minutes.

To Assemble and Plate
Grill tenderloin to temperature preferred. Place crab cake on steak. If made in advance, heat the fritter back up in the oven for a couple minutes before it tops the filet. Serve with mushrooms and asparagus. Drizzle sauce over dish.

The Filet Oscar has become a signature entree for our guests at the Black Watch Steakhouse. The plate combines the best cut of beef with a delicate crispy crab fritter and sauce hollandaise to make for the perfect duo of textures and taste!

PASTA DOUGH

2 cups all-purpose flour, plus more
  for dusting
1 teaspoon salt
3 large eggs plus 1 for egg wash to
  make ravioli
1 tablespoon extra-virgin olive oil
Cornmeal, for dusting

FILLING

2 tablespoons oil
2 chicken legs, with
  thighs attached
2 cloves garlic
1 small onion, diced
2 stalks celery, diced
2 cups Chloe Creek Pinot Noir
4 cups chicken stock
1 sprig fresh thyme
1 bay leaf
1 cup ricotta cheese, whole milk
¼ pound smoked mozzarella
  cheese, grated
2 tablespoons grated
  Parmesan cheese
2 tablespoons chopped parsley
Salt and pepper

RED WINE SAUCE

2 tablespoons extra virgin olive oil
  ¼ pound fresh or frozen porcini
  mushrooms, split in halves
¼ pound fresh porcini mushrooms,
  split in halves
1 large shallot, minced
Reserved braising liquid
  from chicken, about 3 cups
1 sprig fresh thyme
Salt and pepper
2 tablespoons butter, diced

Smoked Chicken Ravioli with Porcini Mushrooms and Red Wine Sauce
4 TO 6 SERVINGS

Preparation of Dough

Combine the flour and salt in an electric mixer with dough hook attachment. Add the eggs and oil and incorporate until it forms a ball. Dust the counter with flour, knead and fold the dough until elastic and smooth, this should take about 5 minutes. Wrap the dough with plastic wrap and let rest for 30 minutes before rolling.

Preparation of Filling

Over medium-high, heat oil in a 2 quart oven safe sauté pan. Season chicken legs lightly with salt and pepper and sear on both sides. Remove chicken from pan and add garlic, onions, and celery and sweat until tender, a little color is okay. Add wine to deglaze pan and reduce until 2 tablespoons of liquid is left. Add chicken stock, thyme and bay leaf and bring to a simmer. Place chicken legs back in the pan, cover with a lid or aluminum foil and place in a preheated 325° oven and braise for two hours until the meat can easily be pulled from the bones. Remove chicken and cool to room temperature. Strain and reserve liquid.

Remove all skin and bones from chicken legs and shred into small pieces. In a mixing bowl, combine the chicken, ricotta, mozzarella, Parmesan, and parsley until incorporated and season to taste. Chill until ready to make ravioli.

Preparation of Ravioli

Beat 1 egg with 1 tablespoon of water to make an egg wash and reserve. Cut the pasta dough in half, cover and reserve the piece you are not immediately using to prevent it from drying out. Dust the counter and dough with a little flour. Form dough into a rectangle and roll through the pasta machine 3 times at the widest setting. Incrementally roll the dough thinner until it is about ⅛-inch thick.

Dust the counter with flour and lay out the long sheet of pasta. Brush surface with the egg wash and place 1 tablespoon of the filling on half of the pasta sheet, about 2-inches apart. Fold the other half of the dough over the filling, making sure all of the filling is covered. With your fingers, gently press out air pockets around each mound of filling. With a sharp knife, cut the ravioli into squares and crimp all edges with the tines of a fork to make a tight seal. Dust the ravioli and a sheet pan with cornmeal to prevent the pasta from sticking and lay them out to dry slightly while assembling the rest.

Cook the ravioli in plenty of boiling salted water for 4 to 6 minutes, or until they float to the top. Lift the ravioli from water with a large slotted spoon and drain in a colander. Do not rinse with water.

Preparation of Red Wine Sauce

Heat half the oil in a medium sauté pan over medium-high heat until almost smoking. Season the porcinis lightly and sear, cut side down, until golden brown. Flip the mushrooms and add the rest of the oil and shallots, and turn the heat down to medium. Sweat the shallots without browning until they are tender, about 5 minutes. Add the braising liquid and fresh thyme and bring to a simmer. Reduce the liquid by half and season to taste.

To Assemble and Plate

Turn off the heat under sauce, add the diced butter and swirl the pan gently until the butter is incorporated. Add strained ravioli to wine sauce and serve.

This is a dish layered with flavors that call out for a Pinot Noir with complexity, balanced acidity and a sophisticated medley of aromatics that echoes the earthy and succulent flavors. The only wine that I can think of that can fill the bill is the 2009 Chloe Creek Russian River Valley Leras Family Vineyard – a match made in heaven.

Coq au Vin
8 TO 10 SERVINGS

MARINADE

24 to 72 hours in advance

1 medium carrot, diced ½ inch

1 onion, diced ½ inch

2 celery stalks, diced ½ inch

1 garlic clove, crushed

1 bottle of Chloe Creek Pinot Noir,
  or enough to cover chicken

1 cup of cognac

1 bouquet garni
  (stuff 1 leek leaf with fresh
  thyme, rosemary and a bay leaf)

Pinch of salt

Pinch of pepper

Pinch herbes de Provence

5- to 6-pounds of chicken pieces

¼ cup olive oil (to cover top)

CHICKEN

½ pound of lardons (lean salted
  lard or bacon, sliced ¼-inch
  widthwise)

3 tablespoons olive oil

4 tablespoons of all-purpose flour

MUSHROOMS

1 tablespoon of olive oil

1 tablespoon of butter

15 to 20 button mushrooms

1 shallot, finely diced

1 tablespoon parsley,
  finely chopped

1 tablespoon of garlic, minced

¼ cup white wine

Salt and pepper

VEGETABLES

1 tablespoon of olive oil

1 tablespoon of butter

Reserved vegetables
  from marinade

1 shallot, finely diced

¼ cup white wine

Salt and pepper

FOR GARNISH

2 tablespoons butter

18 to 20 baby onions, peeled

¼ cup white wine

1 ounce of water

2 tablespoons raw sugar

Preparation of Marinade

Mix all ingredients together in a non-reactive bowl, except the chicken and olive oil. Add the chicken pieces and make sure they are covered completely. Spoon the olive oil on top of the marinade to keep the chicken moist. Let the chicken marinate in the fridge for 24 to 72 hours, mixing occasionally.

Preparation of Chicken

Take the chicken pieces out of the marinade and pat them dry. Strain the marinade, reserving the vegetables and liquid separately. Sauté the lardons in a large oven proof saucepan over medium heat until golden, approximately 5 minutes. Remove the lardons and reserve for the garnish. Keep the melted fat in the saucepan to sauté the chicken until golden, adding in the olive oil. Dust flour over the cooked chicken. Add the marinade liquid and bouquet garni back to the saucepan and bring to a boil. Put in the pre-heated oven at 325° for one hour, or until tender.

When the chicken is almost cooked, start the mushrooms, vegetables and garnish.

Preparation of Mushrooms

Add olive oil and butter to a very hot pan. Sauté the mushrooms and other ingredients for a few minutes until golden. Deglaze with a little white wine and set aside until the chicken is cooked. Add mushrooms to chicken before serving.

Preparation of Vegetables

Add olive oil and butter to a very hot pan. Sauté the vegetables and shallot for a few minutes until cooked and golden. Deglaze with a little white wine and set aside until the chicken is cooked. Add to chicken before serving.

Garnish

Melt the butter in a medium saucepan over high heat. Add the baby onions and sauté for 1 minute. Add the white wine, water and sugar and simmer on low to medium heat until the onions are caramelized, stirring occasionally. Add onions to the chicken just before serving.

To Assemble and Plate

Ladle a hearty portion of this classic dish into a bowl. Serve with crusty bread and a glass of Chloe Creek Pinot Noir.

This classic French chicken stew paired with a medium-body fruit-driven Pinot Noir complements the rich flavors of the dish.

½ bottle red wine to reduce

STEAKS
Four 8-ounce filet mignon steaks
3 tablespoons
Salt and pepper

SWEET CORN HASH
2 tablespoons olive oil
½ white onion, small dice
2 cloves garlic, minced
2 ears sweet corn, kernels removed
2 russet potatoes, peeled and
  medium diced
1½ cups heavy cream
Salt and pepper

Grilled Filet Mignon with Sweet Corn Hash and Red Wine Reduction
4 SERVINGS

Preparation Red Wine Reduction
In a small saucepan, bring the red wine to a boil; reduce the heat until a slow simmer. Further reduce the red wine by three-quarters.

Preparation of Steaks
Rub the filets with a few tablespoons of olive oil. Liberally season filets with salt and pepper and place them on a hot grill, cooking to desired temperature.

Preparation of Sweet Corn Hash
Heat a sauté pan with 2 tablespoons of olive oil and sauté the onion until soft. Add the garlic and cook until fragrant. To this mixture, add the corn kernels, diced potatoes and heavy cream. Bring to a boil and then reduce the heat to a slow simmer. Cook until the potatoes are cooked through and tender, about 10 minutes. The cream should reduce in volume by half. The hash should be thickened from the potato starch. Season to taste with salt and pepper.

To Assemble and Plate
Place the corn hash in the center of the plate. Make a small well in the center of the hash for the grilled filet. Spoon a few tablespoons of the wine reduction around the filet and hash. Serve with sautéed haricots verts if you wish .

Through each season the Adirondacks present an abundant amount of substantial ingredients. It is not the chef that makes a dish great, but the quality of the ingredients that makes a chef.

SHORT RIBS

5 pounds bone-in Buffalo/
  bison short ribs
1 cup olive oil
1 teaspoon kosher salt
1 teaspoon toasted fresh
  ground pepper
1½ cups yellow onion, diced
1½ cups carrot, diced
1½ cups celery, diced
1 cup chopped shallot
1 cup garlic, minced
2 bay leaves
1 bunch thyme sprigs tied together
1 cup Madiera wine
1½ cups Chloe Creek Pinot Noir
1½ cups tomato juice or puree
1 gallon veal stock

MUSHROOM BREAD PUDDING WITH WHITE TRUFFLE

⅓ cup virgin olive oil
2 each shallot, fine diced
3 each fresh morel mushrooms,
  thinly sliced
3 each chanterelle mushrooms,
  thinly sliced
3 each porcini mushrooms,
  ½-inch dice
1 each lobster mushroom,
  ½-inch dice
1 pound day old brioche, cut into
  1-inch cubes
3 eggs, whisked
1½ cups chicken stock or broth
1 cup heavy cream
¼ teaspoon fresh chopped sage
1 teaspoon white truffle paste
Salt and pepper

CRISPY LEEKS

2 leeks, cleaned well
Flour
Salt and pepper
Oil for frying

Braised Bison Short Ribs and Wild Mushroom Bread Pudding with White Truffle
4 SERVINGS

Preparation of Ribs

Remove outer sinews from short ribs and season with kosher salt and fresh ground toasted pepper. Heat olive oil in braising pan or heavy gauge large sauté pan. Brown short ribs on all sides and remove from pan. Add mirapoix of onion, celery, and carrot as well as aromatics consisting of shallots, garlic, bay leaves, and thyme to the pan. Sauté mixture until tender and deglaze with Madiera and Chloe Creek Pinot Noir. Remove all the bits from the bottom of the pan using a wire whisk. Add tomato juice or puree and simmer until the wine reduces by half, and then add the veal stock. Bring to a boil and remove from heat.

Arrange short ribs uniformly in separate braising pan and cover with the veal stock mixture to the top of the short ribs. Cover with foil and braise in a preheated 325° oven for 3 hours.

Remove and cool ribs; the bones should easily slide away from the meat. Remove thyme sprigs and bay leaves. Strain remaining stock and puree remaining mirapoix. Add puree back to remaining stock and simmer on low heat until reduced to desired consistency. Adjust seasoning to taste and reserve hot until serving time.

Preparation of Mushroom Bread Pudding

Heat olive oil in sauté pan. Add shallots and mushrooms. Sauté until tender. Remove mushrooms from heat and cool to room temperature.

Whisk together eggs, chicken stock and heavy cream. Add mushroom mixture, folding gently. Pour mixture over cubed brioche and let stand for 5 minutes. Add truffle paste, sage, salt and pepper, mixing by hand so as not to break the mushrooms any further.

Spray four 6-ounce ceramic cups and divide pudding mixture evenly. Place full cups in a 3-inch high baking dish, fill with water halfway and cover with foil. Bake at 350° for 30 minutes or until done but still moist. Remove from heat and let stand unmolded until service time, or serve immediately.

Preparation of Crispy Leeks

Cut cleaned leeks in half lengthwise, turn over and split lengthwise again; discard dark green parts. Season flour with salt and pepper and dredge leek strips in mixture. Heat enough oil in small pan or deep fryer and carefully drop dredged leeks into hot oil. Fry quickly until lightly browned. Remove and drain. Reserve as garnish.

To Assemble and Plate

Heat the short ribs separately in the oven for 10 to 12 minutes. Remove the bones using kitchen tongs, or your fingers and cover with sauce as desired.

Remove pudding from ramekin and place on serving plate. Remove one portion of ribs and stack in front of pudding. Add a few tablespoons of stock from sauce onto plate. If desired, add some roasted root vegetables alongside the pudding and garnish dish with crispy leeks.

One taste of the Chloe Creek Pinot Noir brought to mind a braised game dish accompanied by side dishes with earthy flavors.

SWEET CORN PUDDING

½ cup sugar

3 tablespoons cornstarch

2 eggs

One 13-ounce can evaporated milk

One 16-ounce can cream corn

Salt and pepper

Nutmeg

FOR FINAL DISH

6 large or 12 medium scallops

6 large leaf greens

2 large fresh tomatoes

Pan-Seared Sea Scallops, Sweet Corn Pudding with Grilled Sturdy Greens and Tomato Confit

6 SERVINGS

Preparation of Pudding

Preheat oven to 350°. Combine sugar and cornstarch in a bowl, and then add eggs, milk and corn. Mix well and pour into individual 3-ounce ramekins and bake 25 minutes or until firm.

Preparation of Tomato Confit

Skin and quarter tomatoes and cook over low heat in sauce pan. Cook tomatoes for 30 minutes.

To Assemble and Plate

In a smoking hot pan, drizzle 2 drops of oil. Season and then sear scallops for 2 to 2½ minutes on each side. Turn ramekin upside down on serving dish. Take fresh greens and lightly oil and grill for a minute or two. Unmold pudding onto serving dish, place green leaf on top of the pudding. Take scallop and set on top of leaf. Drizzle with Tomato Confit.

This was the winning dish I created for Taste of St. Croix.

ROSTI
2 large Yukon Gold potatoes
1 teaspoon salt
1 teaspoon black pepper
4 teaspoons olive oil

Maple-Glazed Venison Loin
One 4- to 6-ounce venison loin
Salt and pepper
1 ounce white wine
3 ounces maple syrup
1½ ounces red wine vinegar
1 ounce unsalted butter
1 ounce demi-glaze*

*Available at specialty and
 gourmet food stores

Maple-Glazed Venison Loin
1 SERVING

Preparation of Rosti
Grate the potatoes and season with salt and pepper. Squeeze the potatoes to remove excess water.

Heat a sauté pan with olive oil and add the potatoes. Slowly raise the temperature until the potatoes are golden brown. Flip the Rosti and finish on the other side. Hold in warm oven until ready to serve.

Preparation of Loin
Season venison loin with salt and pepper. In a sauté pan-sear the venison loin all sides and deglaze with wine. Add maple syrup, vinegar, butter and demi-glaze; reduce to a glaze. The venison should be rare to medium-rare.

To Assemble and Plate
Take a few spoonfuls of glaze and spread on serving dish. Cut venison into serving slices and place on plate intermittently with potatoes. Serve along side another vegetable, like freshly steamed beans.

Venison has rich flavors and needs a young fruit-driven complex Pinot to complement the dish. The ripe wild strawberry flavors in the Pinot Noir pair nicely with the sweetness of the maple glaze.

Four 12-ounce Hereford
  rib-eye steaks

FOR THE TASSO HASH
2 tablespoons neutral oil
2 tablespoons shallot, minced
1 cup Yukon Gold potato, small diced
½ tablespoon of fresh thyme
1 cup tasso, small diced
½ cup beef stock
2 to 4 ounces butter
Salt and black pepper

BLACK GARLIC REDUCTION
4 medium size shallots
2 cups red wine
½ cup balsamic vinegar
2 bay leaves
1 cinnamon stick
4 whole star anise
6 cardamom pods
1 tablespoon whole allspice
3 sprigs rosemary
4 bulbs of black garlic
2 ounces butter
Salt and black pepper

*Available at Asian food stores

Vermont Hereford Beef Rib-Eye with Black Garlic Reduction and Tasso Hash
4 SERVINGS

Preparation for the Tasso Hash
Sweat shallots until translucent in neutral oil. Add diced potato and lightly brown. Add thyme and diced tasso, rendering down slightly. Add about 4 ounces of beef stock and reduce by half to make "gravy." Add butter and reduce further. Salt and pepper to taste and reserve hash.

Preparation for Black Garlic Reduction
In a nonstick skillet, brown shallots. Add red wine and balsamic, along with all spices and herbs. Reduce by half and strain into a new skillet. Add peeled and cleaned black garlic and reduce again by one-quarter and blend until smooth with a hand blender. Add 2 ounces of butter and emulsify. Salt and pepper to taste. Reserve reduction sauce.

To Assemble and Plate
Grill rib-eye steaks until desired temperature. On serving plate, place serving of Tasso Hash and one steak. Drizzle with reduction sauce.

The major driving force for this recipe is geographical; I find this recipe to be very indicative of the flavors and spirit of the northeast at its best.

VEAL

2 pounds veal shanks, cut
  into short lengths
¼ cup all-purpose flour
¼ cup butter
2 cloves garlic, crushed
1 large onion, chopped
1 large carrot, chopped
⅔ cup red wine
2 cups diced tomatoes
⅔ cup veal stock
Salt and pepper

BACON-BRAISED BRUSSELS SPROUTS

1 pound of Brussels sprouts
6 ounces cooked chopped bacon
½ cup brown sugar
¼ cup red wine vinegar
2 tablespoons bacon grease

ROSTI

10 large red potatoes
Olive oil
Salt and pepper
1 tablespoon minced onion
1 tablespoon minced garlic
1 tablespoon fresh chopped parsley
1 tablespoon fresh chopped thyme
1 tablespoon fresh
  chopped rosemary

*Available at specialty and
  gourmet food stores

Veal Osso Buco
4 SERVINGS

Preparation of Veal

Dust the veal shanks lightly with flour. Melt the butter in a large skillet over medium to medium-high heat. Add the veal, and cook until browned on the outside. Remove to a bowl, and keep warm. Add two cloves of crushed garlic and onion to the skillet. Cook and stir until onion is tender. Return the veal to the pan and mix in the carrot and wine. Simmer for 10 minutes.

Pour in the tomatoes and veal stock, and season with salt and pepper. Cover, and simmer over low heat for 1½ hours, basting the veal every 15 minutes or so. The meat should be tender, but not falling off the bone.

Preparation of Brussels Sprouts

Add all ingredients in a medium sauce pan and cook over medium heat 5 to 7 minutes or until sprouts are fork tender.

Preparation of Rosti

Par cook potatoes in water. Peel and grate cooked potatoes. Add onions, garlic and herbs. Heat olive oil until very hot in stoneware or nonstick pan. Add potatoes covering bottom of pan and season. Cook over medium heat about 10 minutes. Flip potatoes using large spatula. Cook 6 to 8 minutes more until browned and tender.

To Assemble and Plate

For each serving, place one veal shank on top of a portion of potatoes. Serve Brussels sprouts along side. Finish dish with few spoonfuls of sauce. Dress dish up with some additions.

I think the richness, depth, and savory characteristics of the slow braised veal shank pairs very well with the nuances found in the Chloe Creek Pinot Noir.

One 8-ounce halibut steak

WATERMELON BRUSCHETTA
3 ounces watermelon, diced
½ ounce red wine vinegar
1 teaspoon olive oil
1 shallot, minced
1 clove garlic, minced
3 leaves basil, freshly chopped

PINOT NOIR POTATO COINS
4 fingerling potatoes
1 teaspoon olive oil
¼ cup onion, diced
1 clove garlic, minced
2 ounces Chloe Creek Pinot Noir
1 teaspoon butter
Salt and pepper

Skillet-Seared Halibut, Watermelon Bruschetta and Pinot Noir Lacquered Potato Coins
1 SERVING

Preparation for Watermelon Bruschetta
In a small mixing bowl combine watermelon, red wine vinegar, olive oil, shallot, garlic and basil. Gently mix together with a serving spoon and salt and pepper to taste.

Preparation for Pinot Noir Lacquered Potato Coins
Boil potatoes in salted water until fork tender and let cool. Slice potatoes in ⅛-inch slices (coins). In a hot sauté pan with olive oil, add potatoes, onions and garlic. Cook until golden brown and then add Pinot Noir and finish cooking until almost all liquid is gone. Add butter, salt and pepper to taste.

Preparation for Halibut
In a smoking hot skillet, add seasoned halibut (Do NOT touch for 2 minutes). Turn fish and cook for another 2 minutes. Remove from heat and let rest for 2 minutes.

To Assemble and Plate
Stack potato coins on serving dish, placing halibut directly on top. Spoon watermelon mixture as an accompaniment.

When preparing the specials for the dining room at Treviso, I always look for the ingredients that are the freshest and in season, such as fresh fruits and vegetables in the summer, hearty squashes and root vegetables in the summer. With this particular dish the sweetness of the watermelon complements the tartness of the Pinot Noir lacquered potato coins. I try to make sure that everything on the plate complements one another and when eaten together, it's a simple medley of flavors in your mouth.

STUFFED VEAL CHOP

Four 18-ounce veal chops, frenched
2 tablespoons blended oil
2 tablespoons butter
8 slices of prosciutto
Four ¼-inch-thick slices
 fresh mozzarella

SALTIMBOCCA SAUCE

1 teaspoon fresh garlic minced
2 tablespoons fresh sage
1 tablespoon chopped
 banana peppers
1 tablespoon chopped red peppers
½ cup red wine
1 cup veal demi-glaze or beef stock*
Salt and pepper

*Available at specialty and
 gourmet food stores

Veal Chop Stuffed with Prosciutto, Fresh Mozzarella and Topped with Saltimbocca Sauce

4 SERVINGS

Preparation of Veal Chops

Make a pocket in the veal chop by making a cut halfway through veal chop. Stuff with prosciutto and fresh mozzarella cheese. Pan-sear in hot sauté pan with light oil and butter. Finish in oven to desired doneness. Take chop out of pan to rest while you make the sauce.

Preparation of Saltimbocca Sauce

In the same sauté pan as the veal chop was cooked, add garlic, fresh sage, banana peppers, red peppers and sauté to lightly brown. Deglaze with red wine and reduce. Add in veal demi-glaze or stock and let reduce until glossy; season with salt and pepper.

To Assemble and Plate

Pour sauce over veal chop and serve with choice of starch and vegetable.

The caramelizing of the hearty veal chop in our rich Demi, along with the sage, plays well with the earthy notes in Pinot Noir.

2 medium onions, thinly sliced

2 tablespoons butter or olive oil

Salt

¼ cup plus pinch sugar

6 fresh figs, cut into thirds
  widthwise

1 pound pizza dough, bought
  or homemade

¼ cup ricotta cheese

½ cup Gorgonzola cheese, divided

1 bunch arugula, divided

4 thin slices prosciutto

Balsamic reduction

Fig and Arugula Pizza
3 TO 4 SERVINGS

Preparation

Caramelize onions by heating butter or oil in a saucepan on medium-high heat. Add onions and stir to coat. Add a pinch of salt and cook 5 minutes. Add a pinch of sugar (optional) and cook until onions brown, approximately 15 minutes. Set aside.

Place pizza stone in oven and preheat to 500°.

Place ¼ cup sugar and pinch of salt in a bowl and mix well. Take cut figs and toss into sugar mixture, coating well. Put sugared figs in heated skillet over medium heat. Cook until sugar caramelizes, about 5 minutes. Turn over and caramelize other side, taking care not to burn. Reserve figs for topping.

Stretch dough into circle. Spread ricotta cheese on top of dough, and then add half of the Gorgonzola. Top with caramelized onions and half of the arugula. Tear prosciutto into 2-inch pieces and place on top of arugula. Add caramelized figs. Place pizza in a 500° oven 15 to 20 minutes. Meanwhile, reduce balsamic.

In a small saucepan over high heat, whisk ½ cup balsamic vinegar constantly until reduced by half. A thick, syrupy consistency is left. Allow to cool.

To Assemble and Plate

Remove pizza from oven and top with the remaining arugula and Gorgonzola. Drizzle with balsamic reduction, and enjoy with a glass of Chloe Creek Pinot Noir.

This pizza was inspired by Chloe Creek Russian River Pinot Noir - being a bit bolder and spicier than the Sonoma. It pairs well with the sweetness of the caramelized figs and the savory of the prosciutto, Gorgonzola cheese and the peppery spice of the arugula.

2½ pounds pork tenderloin
  (trimmed), sliced into
  1½ ounce pieces
1 cup flour, to dredge
3 tablespoons oil
2 shallots pureed
2 cloves garlic, pureed
1-inch fresh ginger, minced
1 tablespoon orange rind,
  finely grated
½ teaspoon sambal
  (Indonesian chili paste)*
1½ teaspoons cumin
1½ teaspoons coriander
¾ cup coconut milk
  (NOT cream of coconut)
½ cup Kecap Manis
  (Indonesian sweet soy)*
Salt and pepper

*Available in Asian or specialty
  food stores.

Babi Kecap
(Pork Tenderloin Bathed in an Exotic Infusion of Indonesian Spices)
6 SERVINGS

Preparation

Dredge the pork slices in flour, shaking off excess. Heat oil in a sauté pan. Sauté pork slices for two minutes on each side until golden brown. Remove pork from pan and set aside. In the same sauté pan add shallots, garlic and ginger cooking until translucent. Add orange rind, sambal, spices and coconut milk. Bring to a boil, stirring, for two minutes. Return the sautéed pork to the pan, add the Kecap Manis and continue cooking 3 to 5 minutes until sauce is reduced and coats the back of a spoon; season with salt and pepper. Serve with Jasmine rice and stir-fry vegetables.

We find Chloe Creek Pinot Noir to be a perfect match for Babi Kecap because of the way the fruit-forward style of its Sonoma fruit melds well with the orange, ginger and coconut milk in the sauce. The silky tannins also lend themselves to the richness of pork tenderloin; overall it's a wonderful pairing.

desserts

CRUMBLE

2 cups flour

2 cups quick cooking oats

1½ cups sugar

1½ cups chopped walnuts

1 teaspoon baking soda

1¼ cups butter, melted

Two 24-ounce cans cherry pie filling

1 cup chocolate chips, optional

MASCARPONE ICE CREAM

(double ingredients to
  make 3 quarts)

Freeze 5 hours

2 large eggs

¾ cup sugar

1 pound mascarpone

1 cup cream

2 cups milk

½ teaspoon salt

Mom's Cherry Crumble
9 TO 12 SERVINGS

Preparation of Crumble

Combine flour, oats, sugar, nuts, baking soda and butter. Mix at low speed until crumbly for 2 to 3 minutes. Reserve 2 cups crumb for topping. Press remaining crumbs into a 9-by-13-inch pan. Bake crust at 350° for 12 to 15 minutes or until lightly browned. Remove from oven and spoon cherry filling over partially baked crust. Sprinkle chocolate chips over cherry filling (optional).

Spread remaining crumbs on top. Bake 25 to 35 minutes or until lightly browned. Serve warm with mascarpone ice cream.

Preparation of Ice Cream

Whisk eggs and sugar until pale in color. Beat in mascarpone until the mixture is smooth. Blend in cream, milk and salt with a whisk.

Freeze mixture in ice cream maker according to manufacturers' instructions. Pack into pints, freeze at least 5 hours.

To Assemble and Plate

Place a warm serving of crumble on a serving dish. Top with a scoop of ice cream or serve alongside.

This recipe matches particularly well with Pinot Noir when finished with the optional chocolate, especially milk chocolate - a lighter chocolate flavor to match the lighter body of the wine. Pinot Noir often exhibits dark fruit flavors, especially cherry, which is a natural match. The full-on richness and fattiness of the mascarpone ice cream provide the perfect contrast or foil for the light tannins and crisp acidity of Pinot Noir. Plus, any excuse for drinking wine with dessert sounds like a perfect pairing to me.

POACHED PEARS

4 pears

1 vanilla bean

750 ml Port wine

1 cinnamon stick

2 cups sugar

CRÈME FRAICHE ICE CREAM

Needs time to freeze

2 cups crème fraîche

2 cups buttermilk

⅓ cup fresh lemon juice

1½ cups sugar

Vanilla-Port Poached Pear with Crème Fraîche Ice Cream
4 SERVINGS

Preparation of Pears

Peel pears. From the bottom slightly hollow out pear to remove seeds with a melon baller. Place in saucepot with scraped vanilla bean, sugar, cinnamon stick, 2 cups sugar and wine. Put on low heat and place a plate on pears to keep them submerged. After 25 minutes check for doneness by poking with a paring knife, if it slides in and out, they are done. Remove pears, and return liquid to stove on medium-high; reduce liquid by half. Pour liquid back over pears and refrigerate.

Preparation of the Ice Cream

Combine lemon juice, crème fraîche, buttermilk, 1½ cups sugar in blender, blend until just combined. Chill. When mixture is very cold, freeze it according to ice cream machine directions.

To Assemble and Plate

Place pear in bowl with one scoop ice cream and pour poaching liquid over all.

This dessert, not being overly sweet, matches beautifully with the full-fruit flavors of Chloe Creek Pinot Noir. Try this recipe in the beginning of autumn when pears are in their peak ripeness.

BREAD PUDDING

2 cups fresh cherries, pitted
 and halved
¼ cup brandy
1 tablespoon cornstarch
1 tablespoon sugar
2½ cups heavy cream
2½ cups milk
1¼ cups sugar
2 teaspoons vanilla
½ teaspoon fresh ground nutmeg
8 large eggs
1 pound brioche, crust removed
 and cubed 1- to 1 ½-inches

STAR ANISE ICE CREAM

Needs time to freeze
2½ cups milk
2½ cups heavy cream
15 egg yolks
1 cup sugar
12 star anise

SPICED MAPLE CARAMEL

8 ounces sugar
2 ounces water
1 teaspoon fresh lemon juice
6 ounces heavy cream
½ vanilla bean
6 ounces maple syrup
Fresh grated nutmeg

Tart Cherry Bread Pudding with Spiced Maple Caramel and Star Anise Ice Cream
10 TO 12 SERVINGS

Preparation of the Bread Pudding

Mix pitted cherries with brandy, 1 tablespoon of sugar and cornstarch, let stand for 1 hour, stirring occasionally.

In a sauce pan, combine cream, milk, sugar, vanilla and nutmeg, heat until hot and sugar is dissolved. Make sure not to boil.

In a large bowl, beat the eggs and slowly add the hot cream mixture, stirring constantly. Add bread to the mixture and lightly fold in, making sure not to crumble the bread too much, allow bread to absorb the custard mixture. Add in the cherry mixture last and fold in just slightly to obtain a marbled effect.

Heat oven to 325°, butter a 10-by-12-inch pan or equal sized baking dish and pour in bread custard mixture, bake until custard is set and top is golden brown and crusty. Allow to cool at room temperature.

Preparation of Ice Cream

Crush star anise coarsely in a spice grinder or with the bottom side of a sauté pan, toast anise in a sauce pan over medium heat. Add milk, cream and sugar to pan and bring to a boil. Remove from heat and allow to slightly cool. Beat egg yolks in a large bowl and slowly add in the cream mixture, whisking the whole time. Cool completely and strain out anise before running in ice cream maker.

Preparation of Spiced Maple Caramel

In a heavy sauce pan, combine the sugar, water and lemon juice, bring to a boil over medium-hign heat, stirring to dissolve the sugar. Cook the sugar to the caramel stage, or if using a candy thermometer 320° to 340°, being very careful towards the end not to get the sugar too dark, as it will go very quickly from "almost ready" to burnt. Color should be a medium brown. At the same time, heat the heavy cream with the vanilla and a small amount of nutmeg, bring to a boil.

When the sugar is at the right color, add in the maple syrup and remove from the heat. Slowly whisk in the heavy cream, being careful of any splatter. Allow to cool at room temperature, but warm up to serve with bread pudding and ice cream.

To Assemble and Plate

Cut serving of bread pudding and place on plate. Top pudding with a scoop of ice cream. Drizzle with caramel.

Dessert is sometimes hard to pair with Pinot Noir, but I thought the tart fruitiness of the cherries along with the spices of this dish worked together nicely with the classic fruit and spice flavors of Pinot Noir.

CHOCOLATE GATEAU

16 ounces.dark chocolate

16 ounces unsalted butter

6 large eggs

12 ounces granulated sugar

6 ounces all purpose flour

3¼ teaspoons baking powder

Fleur de sel*

PINOT NOIR-BLACKBERRY SORBET

Needs time to freeze

Makes 1½ quarts

2 pints blackberries

1½ cups sugar

1 cup Chloe Creek Pinot Noir

2 cups water

CRÈME ANGLAISE

½ cup whole milk

½ cup heavy cream

½ vanilla bean, split

3 large egg yolks

3 tablespoons sugar

*Available at specialty and
gourmet food stores

The tannins found in dark chocolate go so well with the lighter tannins found in a fruity Pinot Noir, so in this sweet presentation we take a sorbet made from Chloe Creek Pinot Noir and pair it with a beautiful French style chocolate cake sprinkled with some Hawaiian sea salt. The pink salt clashes its colors with the red wine sorbet and brings out the deeper chocolate flavors in the gateau. The Crème Anglaise is there to add some creaminess to this decadent dessert. You can make the sorbet and Crème Anglaise the day before baking the gateau and serve them together with the warm chocolate gateau the next day.

Sea Salted Chocolate Gateau with Pinot Noir-Blackberry Sorbet and Crème Anglaise
6 TO 8 SERVINGS

Preparation of Gateau

Preheat oven to 400°. Grease and flour an 8-inch square pan.

Melt the chocolate in a stainless steel bowl over a pot of simmering water. Add butter and stir well to mix completely.

Put the eggs and the sugar in another bowl and whisk until the mixture turns pale and doubles in volume. Add the flour, a tablespoonful at a time, and the baking powder.

Combine the flour mixture with the chocolate mixture, pour into the prepared pan and bake for 30 to 40 minutes or until a toothpick inserted comes out clean.

Place the cake on a cooling rack cool for 15 minutes before turning out and place directly on cooling rack to cool completely.

Preparation of Sorbet

Combine the berries, sugar, wine, and water in a medium pot over medium-high heat stirring occasionally to dissolve the sugar. When the pot comes to a boil reduce the heat and simmer for 15 minutes.

Remove the pot from the heat and pass the mixture through a fine mesh sieve to extract the seeds from the sorbet base.

Chill the sorbet base in the refrigerator completely and then freeze in an ice cream machine following the manufacturer's directions. Transfer the sorbet to a container, cover, and freeze several hours or overnight until firm.

Preparation of Crème Anglaise

Combine and whisk egg yolks and sugar in medium bowl. Gradually whisk hot milk mixture into yolk mixture. Return custard to saucepan and stir over low heat until custard thickens and coats the back of a spoon about 5 minutes, be sure not to boil or the sauce will curdle. Strain sauce through a fine mesh sieve into a bowl. Cover and chill. This can be made 1 day in advance.

To Assemble and Plate

Cut the cake into slices, set them on plates and sprinkle a line of fleur de sel on the cake. Serve with Pinot Noir-Blackberry Sorbet and drizzle with Crème Anglaise.

Camembert with Savory Chocolate Ganache, Cacao Nibs, and Maldon Sea Salt
4 SERVINGS

GANACHE
1 cup of dark chocolate, chopped
1 cup of heavy cream
½ teaspoon of toasted
  ground coriander
½ teaspoon of toasted
  ground allspice
½ teaspoon of cinnamon
Salt

FOR GARNISH
¼ cup cacao nibs*
Maldon sea salt*

*Available at specialty and
  gourmet food stores

Preparation for Chocolate Ganache
Bring chocolate at room temperature for one hour.

Bring heavy cream in a saucepot to a simmer with all three spices. Take cream off of burner and immediately add chocolate. Stir mixture until smooth. Reserve ganache in a warm place to keep pourable.

To Assemble and Plate
With a spoonful of ganache, create a "swoosh" on serving plate by dragging spoon. Take one wedge of Camembert cheese and place upon the ganache. Sprinkle both plate and cheese with cacao nibs and sea salt. Fruit goes nicely with cheese, so add a few thin slices of apple or pear.

The richness of the Camembert and decadence of the chocolate ganache reminds me of a chocolate sundae.

PEAR-APPLE TARTE TATINS

½ cup sugar

3 tablespoons unsalted butter

2 Ginger Gold apples- peeled,
  seeded and cut into 12 slices

2 D'Anjou pears- peeled, seeded
  and cut into 12 slices

¼ teaspoon fresh lemon zest

¼ teaspoon fresh lemon juice

⅛ teaspoon cinnamon

⅛ teaspoon fresh grated nutmeg

1 sheet frozen puff pastry

SPICED WHIPPED CREAM

½ cup heavy cream

2 teaspoons sugar

⅛ teaspoon ground nutmeg

⅛ teaspoon ground cinnamon

⅛ teaspoon ground ginger

Individual Spiced Pear-Apple Tarte Tatins
4 SERVINGS

Preparation of Tarte Tatins
Bring puff pastry to room temperature for 20 minutes.

Preheat oven to 400°. Butter four 8-ounce ramekins and place on baking sheet. Using ramekin as a guide cut 6 puff pastry circles. Cover with plastic wrap and refrigerate until ready to use.

Seed and cut fruit. Toss with lemon zest and juice, cinnamon and nutmeg. Set aside. In a heavy-bottom saucepan over medium-high heat, add butter. When butter is melted, add sugar, stirring to incorporate. Stir with wooden spoon for several minutes until mixture turns a caramel color.

Place 2 tablespoons caramel syrup at bottom of each ramekin. Layer fruit on top and gently press to flatten (makes a better presentation). If any caramel remains, evenly distribute over fruit in ramekins.

Remove the puff pastry discs from refrigerator and cut small slit in center of each. Place one pastry round over fruit in each ramekin, folding under any pastry to cover fruit entirely.

Bake on baking sheet 20 to 25 minutes or until pastry is lightly browned. Allow to cool for 10 minutes.

Preparation of Spiced Whipped Cream
In small bowl, with mixer at medium speed, beat heavy cream, sugar, nutmeg, cinnamon and ginger until stiff peaks form.

To Assemble and Plate
Take serving plate and cover warm ramekin. Gently lift ramekin and invert tarte tatin onto serving plate. Garnish with dollop of whipped cream.

I believe that every book should have a happy ending, so as a foodie, I'll try to hold my own with these exceptional chefs and leave you with one.

Here a classic French upside-down caramelized apple tart is spiced up and given an additional pear component. For an even more decadent dessert, serve with spiced whipped cream. "Happy Endings" from the Editor's kitchen!

PHOTOGRAPHY CREDITS

Remaining photos of dishes sent courtesy of restaurants

Vineyard and winemaking photos courtesy of Bill and Kimberley Comiskey

GLOSSARY OF TERMS

Beurre Blanc/Fondue - Warm white butter rich sauces; typically used on fish

Beurre Manié - Flour and butter kneaded together to a smooth paste; used as thickening agent

Beurre Rouge - Butter based sauce with red wine reduction

Bouquet Garni - Bundle of herbs wrapped in cheesecloth or tied with cooking twine

Braising - To brown or partially cook by dry heat; then to cook covered in small amount of liquid

Butterfly - to split down the center almost through

Caramelize - Process of cooking sugar, including natural sugars in onions, until brown

Chiffonade - To cut into small ribbons

Confit - Term used to describe meat which has been cooked in its own fat and then covered and preserved in the same fat to prevent it from spoiling. For tomato confit: A tomato cooked and covered with olive oil.

Crème Fraîche - Heavy cream cultured to slightly tangy and thickened

Deglaze - To swirl and heat liquid in pan to dissolve particles of food on bottom of pan.

Demi-Glaze - A rich brown sauce or stock reduced by half

Dredge - to sprinkle or coat lightly; typically with seasoned flour or cornmeal

Emulsify - to bind liquids together that typically do not blend smoothly

French Cut Bone - To remove meat, fat and membranes which connect individual rib bones; elegant look

Glacage - A sauce used for glazing

Hollandaise Sauce - classic French master sauce using butter, eggs and lemon juice

Immersion Blender - a handheld appliance to blend ingredients together in the container in which they are being prepared

Julienne - To cut into matchstick strips

Mandoline - A kitchen tool with sharp blades to cut vegetables very thin

Microplane - A kitchen tool for grating

Mirepoix - French name for combination of carrots, celery and onions

Porchetta-style - A boneless, stuffed and rolled roast; typically pork

Remoulade - A sauce typically made with mayonnaise, mustard and herbs

Roulade - Meat or fish, stuffed and rolled

Sauté - To cook food quickly in a small amount of oil in pan over direct medium to medium-high heat

Sweat - To cook over low heat in a small amount of fat

Sweetbreads - Thymus glands of young animals; understood to be veal or lamb

Tasso - Spicy-hot Cajun cured pork

Veal Cheeks - Muscles on either side of the cheekbones; popular French bistro fare

HOW TO MAKE-YOUR-OWN

Balsamic Reduction

Heat balsamic vinegar over medium-high heat, whisking constantly until concentrated, thickened and syrupy. Final product will be 50% of starting volume.

Clarified Butter

Melt unsalted butter over low heat until the butter breaks down into three layers. The white foam should be skimmed off with a spoon. The milk solids will go to the bottom of the saucepan and the yellow middle layer is clarified butter. After skimming all the white foam from the clarified butter, and it has stopped bubbling, remove from heat. Sit butter aside for a few minutes, allowing milk solids to settle to the bottom. Strain the mixture through a fine sieve or cheesecloth. Process typically results in a loss of 25% starting volume.

Rendered Duck Fat

Cut skin and fat from one duck into medium pieces and put in medium-heavy bottomed pan. Add ½ cup water and simmer over medium heat until water evaporates. Strain clear golden fat through sieve.

Stock (Vegetable, Chicken, Beef, Seafood)

A good rule of thumb is to have about half solid ingredients to half water. Vegetables commonly used are carrots, onions, garlic and celery. It's a good idea to throw in some salt, a tablespoon or so of whole black peppercorns and a bay leaf or two for added flavor. Cover your ingredients with the water, bring to a boil and let simmer for about an hour. Cool and strain to remove any pieces of vegetables or scraps. For meat stock, try adding chicken or turkey parts or bones to make stock. Roasting meat, bones and vegetables for about 45 minutes in a 450° oven before adding them to your stock pot along with water, adds flavor. For seafood or fish stock, try adding fish pieces, lobster or shrimp shells and even empty corn cobs.

Vinaigrette

Ratio of oil to vinegar should be 3 to 1. Mix for 10 seconds in a blender. Try mixing lemon juice, mustards, salt, garlic, shallot, herbs or spices, along with extra-virgin olive oil and a vinegar. Basic vinaigrette uses ¾ cup salad oil, ¼ cup white vinegar and salt and pepper to taste. Let stand for 30 minutes for flavors to develop.

starters

49 - Schenectady County Community College Culinary School, Schenectady;
Chef Christopher Tanner
Herbs de Provence Salted Beets

51 - The Turf Club, Saratoga Springs; Chef Rob Cone
Grilled Eggplant, Fresh Mozzarella and Crispy Pancetta Napolean, with Pesto,
Red Pepper Oil and Aged Balsamic

entrees

FISH & SHELLFISH

57 - Angelo's Tavolo, Scotia; Executive Chef Frank Tardio
Pancetta-Wrapped Jumbo Prawn and Pinot Noir Mayonnaise

75 - DUO Modern Japanese Cuisine & Lounge, Saratoga Springs;
Executive Chef-Owner Wilfred Sheng
Seafood Risotto (Wild Sea Shrimp and Lobster, Brown and Black Risotto)

79 - Garden Bistro 24, Colonie; Chef-Owner John Grizzaffi
Prince Edward Island Mussels in a Saffron-Tomato Broth

85 - Inn at Erlowest, Lake George; Executive Chef Ken Lingle
Grilled Georges Bank Swordfish Chop with Celeriac Mousseline, Braised Baby Leeks
and Black Pepper-Pinot Noir Jus

87 - Jack's Oyster House, Albany; Executive Chef Lawrence Schepici
Lobster Louis the Thirteenth

89 - Lake Ridge, Round Lake; Chef Scott Ringwood
Salmon Roulade with Pinot Beurre Rouge

99 - Mirror Lake Inn, Lake Placid; Executive Chef Jarrad Lang
Wild Striped Bass Braised with Red Wine, Mushrooms and Heirloom Tomatoes,
Roasted Fennel and Fingerling Potatoes

103 - New World Bistro Bar, Albany; Executive Chef Ric Orlando
Olive Oil-Poached Salmon with Pinot Noir Sauce

105 - New World Home Cooking, Saugerties; Chef-Owner Ric Orlando
Red Wine Braised Calamari with Mushrooms

106 - Peekamoose Restaurant, Big Indian; Chef-Owner Devin Mills
Pan-Seared Rainbow Trout with Braised Savoy Cabbage and Beurre Fondue

109 - Prime at Saratoga National, Saratoga Springs;
Executive Sous Chef Tim Thompson
Truffle Scallop with Pommes Gratin

121 - Taste, Albany; Executive Chef Paul Ozimek
Coriander-Crusted Tuna, Shoyu Pressed Watermelon, Melted Kumquat and
Avocado Paint

123 - The Bear Café, Woodstock; Chef Eric Mann
Sauteed Atlantic Halibut with Gill Farms Sweet Corn, Toy Box Tomatoes and Leeks

135 - The Turf Club, Saratoga Springs; Chef Rob Cone
Pan-Seared Sea Scallops, Sweet Corn Pudding with Grilled Sturdy Greens and
Tomato Confit

143 - Treviso, Albany; Corporate Chef Ryan Huneau
Skillet-Seared Halibut, Watermelon Bruschetta and Pinot Noir Lacquered
Potato Coins

BEEF & VEAL

69 - Chez Mike, East Greenbush; Chef-Owner Mike Cohen
Filet Mignon "Cheese Steak" Wellington

81 - Gideon Putnam Resort, Saratoga Springs; Executive Chef Brian P. Sterner
Empire Steak (Barrel Cut NY Strip Steak with Cipollini and Shiitake Mushroom Ragout)

83 - Glen Sanders Mansion, Scotia; Executive Chef Will Brown
Grilled Rib-Eye Steak with Garlicky Broccoli Rabe and Tomato-Pepper Jam

110 - Provence, Albany; Executive Chef Michael Cunningham
Beef Bourguignon

117 - Scrimshaw at the Desmond, Albany; Executive Chef Michael St. John
Horseradish-Encrusted Veal T-Bone with Roasted Shallot-Pinot Noir Demi-Glaze

119 - Sperry's, Saratoga Springs; Executive Chef Dale Miller
Veal Sweetbread Cannelloni with Lemony Glacage and Parmesan

125 - The Black Watch Steakhouse, Glens Falls; Chef de Cuisine Nick Yusavage
Filet Oscar

131 - The Interlaken Inn, Lake Placid; Chef Kevin Dunford
Grilled Filet Mignon with Sweet Corn Hash and Red Wine Reduction

132 - The Lake George Club, Lake George; Executive Chef Tony DeStratis
Braised Bison Short Ribs and Wild Mushroom Bread Pudding with White Truffle

139 - The Wine Bar and Bistro on Lark, Albany; Executive Chef Jason Baker
Vermont Hereford Beef Rib-Eye with Black Garlic Reduction and Tasso Hash

141 - The Wishing Well, Wilton; Chef Patrick Longton
Veal Osso Buco

145 - Twenty 8 Tables Restaurant & Bar, Saratoga Springs; Chef-Owner Ron Farber
Veal Chop Stuffed with Prosciutto, Fresh Mozzarella and Topped with
Saltimbocca Sauce

LAMB

93 - Mazzone Hospitality, Albany; Corporate Executive Chef Jaime Ortiz
BBQ Lamb Ribs, Humboldt Fog Ravioli, Matsutake Mushrooms, English Peas and
Smoked Red Beets

95 - MezzaNotte Ristorante, Albany; Chef Mark Graham
Roasted Lamb Rack with Minted Spring Pea Ravioli, Roasted Baby Carrots and
Balsamic Pearl Onions

PASTA

59 - Antipasto's Vegetarian Bistro & Wine Bar, Clifton Park; Owner Steven Zumbo
George Harrison (Fresh Assorted Mushrooms in a Marsala Wine-Porcini Mushroom Demi-Glaze
Sauce over Wild Mushroom Ravioli)

97 - Milano, Latham; Executive Chef Thomas Fitzsimmons
Linguine All'Adriatica

126 - The Brown Derby, Albany; Chef Brian Molino
Smoked Chicken Ravioli with Porcini Mushrooms and Red Wine Sauce

PORK

101 - Miss Sydney's Secret Family Recipes, Albany; Chef AJ Jayapal
Marinated Lucky 7 Pork Chop with Savory Apple-Bacon Waffle, Roasted Parsnips and Chutney Jus

113 - Saratoga National Golf Club, Saratoga Springs; Executive Chef Jason Saunders
Double-Cut Stuffed Pork Chop with Cherry-Walnut Stuffing, Sautéed Haricots Verts and Apple-Brandy Glaze

149 - Yono's, Albany; Certified Executive Executive Chef Yono Purnomo
Babi Kecap (Pork Tenderloin Bathed in Exotic Infusion of Indonesian Spices)

POULTRY & DUCK

61 - Aperitivo Bistro, Schenectady; Executive Chef Courtney Withey
Cornish Game Hens with Fresh Fig and Prosciutto Stuffing, Creamed Spinach, Roasted Cipollini Onions and Grilled Figs

71 - Chianti il Ristorante, Saratoga Springs; Chef Fabrizio Bazzani
Faraona con Pinot e Ciliege (Guinea Hen Porchetta-Style, Filled with Cherries and Pinot Noir for Roasting)

73 - Copperfield Inn Resort, North Creek; Chef Stephen Topper
Duck Leg Confit with Whole-Grain Mustard-Celery Root Slaw

77 - Friends Lake Inn, Chestertown; Chef Matthew Bolton
Strawberry-Thyme Glazed Hudson Valley Duck Breast over Basil Tossed Rice Noodles with Baby Patty Pan Squash

115 - Schenectady County Community College Culinary School, Schenectady; Chef Christopher Tanner
Chicken Braised with Mortadella and Mustard Greens

129 - The Epicurean Bistro & Wine Bar, Latham; Executive Chef Dominique Brialy
Coq au Vin

WILD GAME

63 - Athos, Albany; Executive Chef-Partner Harry Hatziparaskevas
Lago Stefatho (Rabbit Stew)

65 - Beekman Street Bistro, Saratoga Springs; Chef-Owner Tim Meaney
Saba Marinated Quail with Butternut Squash Gratin

67 - Cella Bistro, Schenectady; Chef-Owner Michael Cella
Cinghale all Papparadelle (Wild Boar Ragu over Pappadelle)

91 - Maestro's at the Van Dam, Saratoga Springs; Chef- Owner John LaPosta
Pheasant Fricassee

137 - The Whiteface Club & Resort, Lake Placid; Chef Richard Brosseau
Maple-Glazed Venison Loin

PIZZA

147 - Village Pizzeria and Ristorante, Middle Grove; Chef-Owner Sandra Foster
Fig and Arugula Pizza

desserts

153 - Cella Bistro, Schenectady; Chef-Owner Michael Cella
Mom's Cherry Crumble

155 - Chez Mike, East Greenbush; Chef-Owner Mike Cohen
Vanilla-Port Poached Pear and Crème Fraîche Ice Cream

157 - Mirror Lake Inn, Lake Placid; Executive Chef Jarrad Lang
Tart Cherry Bread Pudding with Spiced Maple Caramel and Star Anise Ice Cream

159 - Schenectady County Community College Culinary School, Schenectady;
Chef Christopher Tanner
Sea Salted Chocolate Gateau with Pinot Noir-Blackberry Sorbet and Crème Anglaise

161 - The Wine Bar and Bistro on Lark, Albany; Executive Chef Jason Baker
Camembert with Savory Chocolate Ganache, Cacao Nibs and Maldon Sea Salt

163 - Happy Endings from the Editor, *Chloe Creek Pinot Pairings*; Angela J. Chichester
Individual Spiced Pear-Apple Tarte Tatins